# Parenting and Inclusive Education

# Parenting and Inclusive Education

## Discovering Difference, Experiencing Difficulty

Chrissie Rogers
*Keele University, UK*

palgrave
macmillan

First published 2007 by
PALGRAVE MACMILLAN
Houndmills, Basingstoke, Hampshire RG21 6XS and
175 Fifth Avenue, New York, N.Y. 10010
Companies and representatives throughout the world

PALGRAVE MACMILLAN is the global academic imprint of the Palgrave Macmillan division of St. Martin's Press, LLC and of Palgrave Macmillan Ltd. Macmillan® is a registered trademark in the United States, United Kingdom and other countries. Palgrave is a registered trademark in the European Union and other countries.

ISBN-13: 978–0–230–01880–8    hardback
ISBN-10: 0–230–01880–7    hardback

This book is printed on paper suitable for recycling and made from fully managed and sustained forest sources. Logging, pulping and manufacturing processes are expected to conform to the environmental regulations of the country of origin.

A catalogue record for this book is available from the British Library.

A catalog record for this book is available from the Library of Congress.

10   9   8   7   6   5   4   3   2   1
16   15   14   13   12   11   10   09   08   07

Printed and bound in Great Britain by
Antony Rowe Ltd, Chippenham and Eastbourne

*For Sherrie*

# Contents

# List of Tables and Boxes

# Acknowledgements

Primarily I owe gratitude to all the parents involved in this research for sharing their private lives with me. Without this group of people the research would not have been possible, or as colourful! I would like to acknowledge the support of the Economic and Social Research Council (R42200034354) (PTA-026-27-0563). Without their support I would have been a very poor postgraduate student and postdoctoral fellow. I would also like to acknowledge that the *British Journal of Sociology of Education* has already published a paper by me and that small parts reappear here in this book.

I cannot thank Helen Lucey and David Morgan enough for their academic support and critical engagement with this work. They have been superb critics in aiding me to think through the final workings. I would like to thank both Jane Hindley and Pam Cox for their supervisory support during the PhD research, and Jackie Turton and Catherine Will for commenting on work in the early stages and listening to my insecurities. Thanks also to Ian Craib, Jane Ribbens McCarthy, Ken Plummer, Martin Richards, Nigel South and the 'Women's Workshop', who have all inspired or supported me in one way or another during the PhD and postdoctoral days.

I would also like to thank all those who have helped me to realise there's more to life than a PhD and academic research (not that I really needed much persuasion!) – to name a few; Ray Rogers (my Dad), Jacqueline Campion, Jackie and Graham Tuckwell, Helen Scott, Elaine Rogers and all my friends. However, my Mum, Shirley Rogers, has been the rock during all of this hard work.

Deepest thanks go to Eamonn Carrabine (fortunately also an academic!). He has listened to me go on about my work, my daughter and her related teenage angst. He has read and commented on earlier drafts and been there for me always. Significantly, he became my best friend, drinking partner, confidant and husband, and has supported me in all things related to my daughter and my academic life.

This research is, of course, dedicated to my daughter, Sherrie, who has been part of the narrative and listened to my never-ending, 'not now I'm working'. I hope that for a short while at least, I can now say, 'sure let's do it', before the next academic deadline kicks in!

Even with all this support, any comments I've chosen to ignore, and any mistakes that are evident in this book are of my own doing. Scarily for good, and for bad, only I can be solely responsible for the finished work.

# List of Abbreviations

| | |
|---|---|
| AD/HD | Attention deficit/hyperactivity disorder |
| AS | Asperger's syndrome |
| ASD | Autistic spectrum disorder |
| BSA | British Sociological Association |
| DES | Department of Science |
| DfEE | Department for Education and Employment |
| DfES | Department of Education and Skills |
| DLA | Disability living allowance |
| EBD | Emotional and behaviour difficulties |
| EP | Educational psychologist |
| GCSE | General Certificate of Secondary Education |
| IEP | Individual education plan |
| IQ | Intelligence quotient |
| LEA | Local education authority |
| LSA | Learning support assistant |
| MLD | Moderate learning difficulties |
| MMR | Measles, Mumps and Rubella |
| nasen | National association of special educational needs |
| NUT | National Union of Teachers |
| OCD | Obsessive compulsive disorder |
| OFSTED | Office for standards in education |
| OPCS | Office of population, census and surveys |
| PDD | Pervasive developmental disorder |
| PRU | Pupil referral unit |
| SATs | Statutory assessments tests/tasks |
| SEN | Special educational needs |
| SENCO | Special educational needs coordinator |
| SENT | Special educational needs tribunal |
| SLD | Severe learning difficulties |
| SPLD | Speech and language difficulties |
| UPIAS | Union of the physically impaired against segregation |

# 1
# Introduction

Because I wanted it to be right this time and I suppose what it was is you have this fairy tale in your mind, where you get married and you have a baby and you push a pram around and you are going to have this beautiful baby that is gorgeous and lovely and cooing and all that, and it's just an illusion and it's just something that little girls have and then that illusion was shattered ...

(Kim, son with cerebral palsy)

Maybe it [anti-depressants] would have helped me get through my depression quicker, I don't know. To me it's like no matter what drug I take I've still got the problem to deal with at the end of it. ... But I've always liked to drink, but I went heavy at it ... I hated coming home ... I hated going to work ...

(Neil, son diagnosed with autistic spectrum disorder)

I think it was so hard to be a parent of a child with special needs ... you don't really know what to expect, you don't really know what to look for ... and it's emotionally traumatic ... you've got to *think* your child's different ... I think that parents; ... if their child's in mainstream school, their child's less different.

(Stella, son diagnosed with a 'brain disorder', possibly on the autistic spectrum)

When we went to a birthday party a little girl got scratched on the eye, quite badly actually. He really did scratch her ... the mother went absolutely berserk, and I was standing there trying to reason with her and say, 'you know I'm really sorry', and, 'my son has a speech and language problem, and he can't hear very well ... and he has a problem with children around him', and she was saying things like, 'well that's not my problem that's yours'. Then I discovered I was struggling at this point trying to fight back the tears, trying to be in control, bearing in mind there were about 30 people standing around me all silent and her screaming at me.

(Kerry, two sons, one with verbal dyspraxia and the other possibly dyspraxic)

[Speaking about mainstream education] I don't agree with it at all for children with speech and language problems, particularly with receptive disorders, because ... they barely understand what the teacher is saying.
(Tina, daughter with speech and language difficulties)

As a member of the audience and a presenting delegate, I wait for the conference to begin. This particular one only happens every five years so is a big event for academics and education practitioners. The Inclusive and Supportive Education Conference (ISEC, 2005) is called 'Inclusive Education: Celebrating Diversity?' The opening ceremony begins and the room is filled with music and young people on the stage performing their interpretation of 'inclusive education'. They weave in and out, their bodies supple and mobile, their voices clear and their story profound. They sing and chant 'seize the day!' at the end of punctuated exclamations of 'individuality', 'sharing', 'creativity', 'SUCCESS!' A lump in my throat and a tear attempts to escape. I pretend I have something in my eye and look around to see if I'm the only one emotionally provoked. Either I was, or like me, everyone else was able to disguise his or her emotionality. This, after all is a serious event. I recall my daughter being on stage desperately trying to remember a

line, and me willing her to ... whatever ... she was
great. Back in the audience I'm sad and angry. I know
that the philosophical underpinning of inclusive education is in some way right, or is it I ponder ... but
anyway is it not a little premature to celebrate it, when
we haven't got there? I go back to my room and cry,
for myself and for my daughter who will always be
different and indeed difficult? I think about how the
researcher and her self have merged: how I often go to
conferences, as a sociologist and end up reflecting on
my position as a mother.

(Personal research notes, 2005)

## Introduction

These windows into parents' lives capture just a snapshot of the dilemmas of becoming (and being) a mother or father with a 'disabled' child,
as well as telling us something about policy discourse and practice within
the context of social inclusion and, more specifically, 'inclusive' education. The stories that unfold in this book, from the very beginning, aim
to capture in depth what it is like to mother a child with impairments
and, more specifically, a child identified with 'special' educational needs
(SEN), in a British context, with a view to contribute to debates on parenting, disability and education. What this book actually does is not only
capture these sensitive parental narratives, but also create a sociological
space to discuss in depth, issues about dealing with difficulty and, specifically, learning disability at both a theoretical and experiential level.

   This research developed out of a desire to examine conflict and contradiction within education policy and how children identified with SEN
were assessed and provided for. This concern arose from my own difficult experiences with mothering a learning disabled child, the education
process and changes in education policies. While education policy and
practice remained a central focus in the research, it became obvious as
I carried out interviews with parents that their personal experiences of
mothering were the driving force. The education process became secondary in relation to the mothers' and fathers' narratives, but it is so
embedded in their experiences as their child reaches school age that it
is difficult to separate the two.

   With the above in mind, I have concentrated on gaining a picture of
the whole experience of mothering an impaired child from pregnancy

through to young adulthood. Not all the children in this study have reached adulthood yet, but listening to mothers and fathers who have been through and are going through this mothering journey has enabled me to obtain life course data. In addition to this, the actual interview process was in-depth and informal. It engaged with questions about parents' experiences, from how they felt about the birth of their child, their expectations and initial reactions to a diagnosis of impairment, to dealing with the transformation of their lives, including changing social relations and career prospects. Some of the parents in this research still have young children and are at the beginning of their mothering journey. Others, like myself, have young adults and can reflect on the education and social process so far.

## Laying the foundations

Becoming a mother, or mothering (I use the term 'mothering' to describe a culturally recognised gendered role, but some fathers also take on a significant mothering role), a learning impaired child dramatically changes the expected horizon of what becoming a mother involves, her public performance and her private internal *and* external dialogues. Expectations of a certain norm – whether that is celebrating a birth, maternal bonding, returning to work, a child's healthy body, speech and language, hearing, sight, socially appropriate behaviour, academic ability, mainstream schooling, for example – means that some of the above expectations are shattered and the expectations of a normative life course are changed forever. Moreover (especially in the Western world), mothering has been explicitly associated with a private and personal life but has become publicly surveyed by health and education professionals. This process has not necessarily been driven by 'the professional', but by wider public policy and political and cultural discourses.

This book is based on the stories of 24 parents, all of whom have children identified with (or were in the process of being identified with) SEN. Definitions of SEN in England and Wales are based on a 'greater difficulty in learning than the majority of children of his age', or 'he has a disability which either prevents or hinders him from making use of educational facilities of a kind generally provided for children of his [*sic*] age in schools within the area of the local education authority' (DfEE, 1996). This book is peppered with some of my experiences in an attempt to merge my biography with the parents' stories, but what also emerges is the 'sociological imagination' that is widely referred to when discussing such matters as 'the personal troubles of milieu' and 'the public issues of social structure'. This distinction, according to Wright Mills (1959: 8), 'is an essential tool of the sociological imagination and a feature of all classic work in social science'. He suggests that the sociological imagination is brought to life by distinguishing between the personal and public, the micro world of experienced everyday life and the public issues that form part of the macro social world.

By studying the personal and private lives of individuals, questions and answers about the broader social picture – in this case, mothering, impairment, learning disability and SEN – can be asked and addressed. For example, we can address public issues about education policy and provision, social services, the medical profession and family practices. We can also address personal and private troubles about mothering, emotional angst, mental health and coping mechanisms. Importantly, concepts such as disappointment, denial and exclusion are drawn on and referred to in analysing such qualitative data and policy documents. Significantly, the two aspects of the private and public spheres experientially merge.

The private and personal narratives are the most important part of this research, as is the *telling* of intimate stories (Plummer, 1995). Certainly the stories in this book are an intimate window into lives lived. But the private world has often been mistaken for something that can only be studied psychologically or psychoanalytically, although the private world (experience) is an emotional response to the social world in relating it to the self and well-being. This is experienced both personally and in relation to the public self. My understanding of the private, personal and public has been aided not only by Wright Mills, but also by feminist researchers such as Ribbens and Edwards (1998). Women researchers have had to face criticism about their involvement and subjectivity when researching issues close to their hearts but continue to suggest, '[t]he central dilemma for us as researchers is that we are seeking to explore such privately based knowledges and personal understandings, but to then reconstitute them within publicly based disciplinary knowledge' (ibid.: 13).

## Introducing disability

Throughout this book I deliberately use the word 'impaired/impairment' rather than 'disability', when referring to a child's condition, in order to stress an important analytical distinction. Impairment, as defined by the Union of the Physically Impaired Against Segregation (UPIAS) is 'the lack of a limb or part thereof or a defect of a limb, organ or mechanism of the body' (Oliver, 1996: 22). Disability is said to be 'a form of disadvantage which is imposed on top of one's impairment, that is, the disadvantage or restriction of activity caused by a contemporary social organization that takes little or no account of people with physical impairments' (ibid.).

Children's impairments are often problematised (Armstrong and Barton, 1999) and can be categorised in the Foucauldian sense (Foucault, 1973, 1980), but *experiencing* disability, according to Oliver (1996), is a result of social construction within a social model of disability. The parents I interviewed report that they experience both the actual difficulties that come with dealing with an impairment on a day-to-day basis and the disability via cultural and political spheres that feeds into these day-to-day experiences. It is an interrelated experience merging personal experiences or responses to childrearing in adversity, and the external forces of disablism within the cultural and political spheres, based upon disadvantage and social/cultural perception. An important point to make here is that there are *actual* difficulties experienced by the parents that are directly related to their child's impairment and associated problems, *but* that the parents also experience disability as a social construction.

There are a growing number of medical and psychological terms for different kinds of impairments, such as Asperger's syndrome (AS), attention deficit/hyperactivity disorder (AD/HD), autistic spectrum disorder (ASD), cerebral palsy, Down's syndrome, dyslexia, dyspraxia and speech and language difficulties (SPLD), to name a few. Some children are classified as having low intelligence and others as having high intelligence. These labels in themselves may or may not be useful when it comes to the education of a child who has been diagnosed or identified with such impairments, but all the same, they can influence the inclusion/exclusion of the child (as too can the actual physiological/learning impairment).

The family can also be 'disabled', as a child's impairment often means the family is excluded and marginalised from certain social activities (Barnes et al., 1999; Gray, 2002). The mother, too, can become practically and emotionally 'disabled' in her new role as a mother with an impaired child (Baldwin and Carlisle, 1999). This is similar to those who have been diagnosed with a terminal illness (Sontag, 1991) or have sustained or developed a physical disability (Morris, 1991; Slack, 1999). The families in this research are a combination of single mothers or fathers, dual parents, mothers and stepfathers, siblings or only child; but all have in common a child or children with impairment in the family. However the family is formed, they are all 'disabled'.

## Locating recent past and current policies

In carrying out this research and writing this book, it is important, because of the context within which the mothers and fathers who have participated in my research live – that of inclusive education policy and directives – to contextualise the policy discourse: the political sphere. 'The Warnock Report' (DES, 1978) defined SEN positively by dismissing the use of labels such as 'imbecile', 'feebleminded', 'maladjusted' and 'educationally sub-normal' and began to work on a continuum of need where children would be able to access mainstream education and work alongside their peers, with a greater involvement of the parents. (I realise 'need' is a subjective term and often dependent on the professional identifying it. However, for the present purpose I continue to use the framework of SEN as it remains within the narratives of both the parents and the professionals.)

The Warnock Report found that although only 2 per cent of school-age children had educational difficulties that affected them so severely that they could only be educated in a special school, 18 per cent were found to have some educational difficulties but were clustered in the bottom sets or placed in remedial classes within mainstream schools. The Warnock committee recommended (and it was agreed) that special help and protection was necessary for children with difficult or complex SEN. As a result of the report, it was suggested that certain children may need a statement of SEN, a formal process of identification and assessment in an attempt to highlight their difficulties and therefore make provision for those children. The Education Act 1981, which came into effect in 1983 (influenced by the Warnock Report), was based on the identification and assessment of a child's needs in order to make suitable provision for the education of all children.

The 1981 Education Act changed the whole concept of SEN. Special educational 'needs' replaced special educational 'treatment'. This was a conscious move to disregard the idea that learning difficulties and/or emotional and behavioural difficulties (EBD) were medical problems and therefore treatable. Instead, the emphasis lay on the individual needs of each child and on his or her educational potential. I would not dispute the educability of every child (in one form or other), however; this move from an impairment that is treatable to the education *potential* of a child means that education is placed above 'treatment' of an impairment such as physiotherapy, speech and language therapy or sensory therapy. A series of policy documents over the following years were introduced restructuring the education system. All mainstream schools were to provide education for children with SEN where possible. The emphasis was on 'where possible' and has been the loophole in excluding children with SEN since the 1980s.

In 1988 the Education Reform Act centralised power in the then Department of Science (DES) and invoked a national requirement for all children to reach certain academic standards at certain stages. This reform had a dramatic effect on SEN with the introduction and enforcement of the National Curriculum – which supported a homogeneous teaching structure. Children with different types of abilities would follow a similar, if not the same, curriculum nationally, and it was agreed that where possible children with SEN should have access to it. This meant that performance could then be tabled and inter- and intra-school competition encouraged. Nationally, levels of ability could be charted and a homogeneous curriculum could be followed. However, this does not allow for individuality or diverse and different abilities.

Maclure (1992: v) considers the 1988 Education Reform Act as by far the most important piece of education legislation since the Education Act of 1944. He argues that it changed the 'basic power structure of the education system'. The power that was once localised in local education authorities (LEAs) moved to central government, increasing the responsibility of the Secretary of State for Education and Science. The result was that the role of the LEAs in education had limitations in and around the whole structure of provision and they were in fact duty bound to give 'greater autonomy to schools and governing bodies' (ibid.).

Centralised power invoked a national requirement to reach certain academic standards at certain stages and ages. The 1988 Education Reform Act and the National Curriculum has encouraged

- Competition between schools and the public tabling of performances and targets.
- The charting of levels of ability.
- A homogeneous curriculum that could be followed by all children.

Since New Labour came to power in 1997 they have built on the previous government's policies. Raising educational standards has been prioritised, and this is reflected in educational policies within a discourse of high academic achievement and league tables. There are slightly less stringent requirements now for children with SEN to follow the National Curriculum rigidly. In certain cases, however, there are still fearsome debates around who should have access to it and that all children should have it available to them.

Other government directives include the *Excellence in Schools: White Paper* (DfEE, 1997b), in which raising British educational standards has been paramount. No one would dispute the aim of raising standards, but along with this are 'Oscar'-like rewards for teaching performance, zero tolerance for under-performance, league tables and the privileging of examination results. Here there is a clear conflict between inclusion and school performance. The pressure to sit and pass exams is experienced by parents via their children's experiences and education professionals' actions, as highlighted by Benjamin (2002: 43). 'Attention is focussed on the numbers and percentages of students scoring five or more passes at C grade or above, since this is the "expected level" and the benchmark for externally recognised success. It is also the measure used in compiling local league tables.' She goes on to reveal an example of this in a school staff room.

> Dave passes round the list of results from the top point-scorer to those who have scored no points at all. The room is full of exclamations – 'I knew she could do it!' 'Only three C's for Zina!' [...] I turn straight to the last page to see if Cassandra got any grades. She didn't get English Literature (which is no surprise) but she got an F in textiles. No one else on my row seems interested in the last page.
>
> (ibid.)

Not only are General Certificates of Secondary Education (GCSEs) grade C and above the externally recognised pass mark in England and Wales, it would seem that there are pressures to eliminate anything that may interfere with the efficient running of the education process, which has a negative impact on the inclusion of impaired children with SEN.

Furthermore, the Code of Practice (DfES, 2001a), the Education Act 1996 (DfEE) and the Special Education Needs and Disability Act (DfES, 2001b) all make up guidance or legislative directives for educating children with SEN. The last of these is supposed to bring together the SEN part of the 1996 Act and the Disability Discrimination Act 1995. Part 1 of the 2001 Act

- Strengthens the right of children with SEN to be educated in mainstream schools where parents wish it and where the interests of other children can be protected.
- Requires LEAs to ensure that parents of children with SEN are provided with advice and information and a means of resolving disputes with schools and LEAs.
- Requires LEAs to comply, within prescribed periods, with orders of the SEN tribunal (SENT), and makes other technical changes in support of the SENT appeals and statementing processes.

- Requires schools to inform parents where they are making SEN provision for their child, to allow schools to request a statutory assessment of a pupil's educational need.

Part 2 of the Act amends the Disability Discrimination Act 1995 by assigning new duties to providers of school and post-16 education. This is intended to ensure that within education there should now be reasonable adjustments made to accommodate children with impairments. While Lindsay (2003) points to the fact that one of the previous caveats has been lost, in the main it seems what is described is no different, in effect, to what is stipulated in the caveats of the previous Education Act with regard to SEN and therefore will not necessarily ease the process for families and carers.

These documents explicitly suggest that the education of children identified with SEN should take place within the *mainstream* setting and that *parental involvement* is strongly encouraged. Alongside this move towards mainstream education is a push for higher academic standards and specialist schooling where specific skills are prioritised and honed. That is to say, privileging academic certification and creaming off children in specific areas of expertise. Parents' rights, children's rights and teachers' rights often conflict, and can cause tension, dissatisfaction and difficulty. It is the *parents* that this research concentrates on as they live within this policy context.

## Introductions: the parents and a research process

Between March 2001 and November 2002, and in May 2003 I carried out 40 unstructured interviews with 24 parents (21 mothers and 3 fathers) in the south of England. All the parents had one or more child or young adult aged between 4 and 19 with one or more of the following impairments: ASD; AS; Down's syndrome; cerebral palsy; AD/HD; a 'rare' syndrome; learning disabilities; dyslexia; dyspraxia; speech, language and/or communication difficulties; hearing impairment; visual impairment; medical problems such as epilepsy, hole in the heart or bowel problems; obsessive compulsive disorder (OCD) and EBD.

I relied on the snowball method – which resulted in the parents coming from one type of ethnic group: white British. No black or ethnic minorities came forward when I asked for participants at any observation sites or in the school newsletter. Moreover, I do not recall a great ethnic mix at the participant observation sites nor at the school where the newsletter was sent. In addition, my own social networks were, as such, that I did not know anyone of an ethnic minority with an impaired child. This is problematic in gaining ethnic diversity, but it also indicates there may be an absence of ethnic minorities in these particular places due to the set-up of user groups at the conferences I attended. I interviewed six parents who have *two or more* impaired children aged 5–18 years, six parents who have impaired children aged 4–8 years, six parents who have impaired children aged 11–14 years and six parents who have impaired teenagers aged 15–19 years. Fifteen parents were working class and nine middle class. For a fuller illustration of the parents, see Table 1.1.

### 'It's all a bit easy' (or not!): issues of access

As a mother of a teenager with impairments I realised that my position handed me an 'insider' role very early on. This was based on our shared identity as parents of an impaired child identified with SEN. While this assisted my ability to access respondents, both professionals and parents, it was often difficult to negotiate the role. Our shared knowledge about particular difficulties and dealing with professionals meant at times there were questions left unasked or comfortable silences and nods of the head as described here:

> Lynne talks about her difficulties in dealing with 'experts' language tells me, 'I can remember saying to the speech therapist it's as if I'm talking a different language and he has to repeat it because he's translating it. Know what I mean?' 'Yeah ...' I reply. [Lynne, Pp 2]. If I did not know what she meant, or I was not so 'involved' in the conversational process then maybe I would have said to her, and many of my participants, 'No I do not, could you explain please?' Or 'yes I do but could you explain what you mean?' Neither of which happened. Is that so bad? If I was not an insider then it is possible that my participants would not have got to the point of even suggesting I knew what they meant, and it would have been a different experience for example if a researcher without children had been conducting the research.
>
> (Rogers, 2003: 52)

Contacts with my daughter's education professionals helped in gaining participants via the snowball method. I also gained participants from the conferences I attended. After my research had begun, on a few occasions I attended a coffee morning at my daughter's school with a view to gaining respondents and carrying out participant observation. However, I did not obtain any participants as I got more from these groups as a

*Table 1.1*  Interview grids

**Interview Grid: Table (a), Mothers (father) with <u>more than one</u> child with impairments. School year at the time of interview, Reception–Post 16**

| Name | Jack | Trisha | Tracy | Kathy | Marlene | Kerry |
|---|---|---|---|---|---|---|
| **Interview (s)** | 1: 01/11/01 | 1: 13/05/02 | 2: 10/05/02, 20/05/03 | 1: 02/05/02 | 2: 08/06/01, 7/01/02 | 6: 13/03/01–22/07/02 |
| **Year of birth** | 1950s | 1961 | 1968 | 1963 | 1967 | 1964 |
| **Partnership status** | Divorced | Married | Divorced/living with partner | Married | Separated | Separated |
| **Class position** | Working class | Working class | Working class | Working class | Working class | Working class |
| **Paid employment** | None | Part-time cleaner/domestic | None | Bank (casual) Nurse | None | Full-time studying |
| **Impaired child's age at the first interview** | 18 and 15 | 15 and 11 | 15 and 10 | 13 and 11 | 11, 7 and 6 | 7 and 5 |
| **Children's combined impairments at the time of interview** | MLD and medical problems | Severe dyslexia, dyscalculia and dyslexia | Hydrocephalus, cerebral palsy and a rare syndrome | Dyslexia | AD/HD, AS, speech and language problems, OCD and visual impairment | Verbal dyspraxia, AD/HD? |
| **Access point** | Daughters networks | nasen conference | Sister of an acquaintance | Infocus/ LEA parents evening | Snowball from the Afasic conference | Friend |

Interview Grid: Table (b), Mothers (father) with one child with impairments. School year at the time of interview, Pre-school–Year 3

| Name | Mary | Tina | Brenda | Neil | Trinny | Christine |
|---|---|---|---|---|---|---|
| Interview(s) | 2: 08/06/01, 22/05/03 | 2: 28/06/01, 22/05/03 | 1: 04/06/01 | 2: 27/07/01, 27/09/02 | 1: 13/05/02 | 2:04/06/01, 22/05/03 |
| Year of birth | 1965 | 1959 | 1963 | 1960 | 1967 | 1954 |
| Partnership status | Married | Married | Married | Married | Single | Second marriage |
| Class position | Middle class | Middle class | Working class | Middle class | Middle class | Working class |
| Paid employment | P/t lecturer at University | F/t accountant and helpline volunteer for one session a week. | None | Primary school teacher | Part-time management consultant | Part-time civil servant |
| Impaired child's age at the first interview | 8 | 7 | 5 | 5 | 4 | 4 |
| Child's impairment/s at the time of interview | AD/HD and AS or ASD | SPLD and dyspraxia. | SPLD | ASD | ASD | ASD |
| Access point | Afasic conference 2001 | Afasic conference 2001 | nasen conference 2000 | Afasic conference in 2001 | Infocus/LEA parents evening | nasen conference |

(Continued)

*Table 1.1* (Continued)

**Interview Grid: Table (c), Mothers with one child with impairments. School year at the time of interview, Year 6–Year 9**

| Name | Karen | Merl | Debbie | Kat | Stella | Francis |
|---|---|---|---|---|---|---|
| Interview(s) | 3: 12/09/01, 25/07/02, 27/03/03 | 1: 14/05/02 | 1: 23/05/02 | 1: 20/06/02 | 1: 20/11/01 | 1: 14/05/02 |
| Year of birth | 1953 | 1958 | 1955 | 1962 | 1950 | 1955 |
| Partnership status | Divorced | Married | Married | Married | Divorced | Married |
| Class position | Working class | Middle class | Middle class | Working class | Working class | Middle class |
| Paid employment | None | None | Casual care work | Inclusion manager | None | Sister and nurse trainer |
| Impaired child's age at the first interview | 13 | 14 | 13 | 13 | 11 | 12 |
| Child's impairment/s at the time of interview | Down's syndrome | EBD | Dyspraxia, dyslexia and AS? | Dyspraxia | Brain disorder and possible ASD | AD/HD or AS |
| Access point | MLD school | Infocus/LEA parents evening | Ante-natal classes (1986) | Snowball | MLD school newsletter | Infocus/LEA parents evening |

**Interview Grid: Table (d), Mothers (father) with one child with impairments. School/college year at the time of interview, Year 10–Post 16**

| Name | Katy (with husband) | Una | Lynne (with partner) | Kim | Tim | Babs |
|---|---|---|---|---|---|---|
| Interview(s) | 1: 07/05/02 | 1:20/08/01 | 1: 06/03/02 | 3: 02/04/01–04/11/02 | 1: 10/05/02 | 2: 30/04/02, 18/11/02 |
| Year of birth | Early 1960s | 1950s | 1952 | 1965 | 1947 | 1949 |
| Partnership status | Married | Married | Second partnership | Second marriage | Married | Married (had a two year separation) |
| Class position | Working class | Middle class | Middle class | Working class | Working class | Working class |
| Paid employment | Part-time dinner lady | Parent advocate | Data access manager | Fire-fighter | Retired at 52 | None |
| Impaired child's age at the first interview | 19 | 18 | 18 | 15 | 16 | 15 |
| Child's impairment/s at the time of interview | AS | ASD, semantic pragmatic disorder and severe dyspraxia. | AS and epilepsy | Cerebral palsy and hearing impairment | Down's syndrome | AS and epilepsy |
| Access point | Infocus/LEA parents evening | Afasic conference 2001 | Snowball | Friend of a friend | Acquaintance of a friend | Infocus/LEA parents evening |

parent, rather than as a researcher, and needed to access the group for my own personal reasons. Instead, I asked the head teacher to put a request for participants in the school newsletter. That way parents were able to make a decision about participating without feeling under pressure.

As a mother of a child identified with SEN I became a member of nasen (the national association of special educational needs). They hold an annual exhibition that usually spans three days in central London. I attended this exhibition in November 2000 and 2001. I did gain some participants via this route; however, being involved in the workshops as an observer informed the research significantly. To demonstrate this, here are some snapshots from my field notes written immediately after I left a seminar on *'inclusive practices within the mainstream classroom'*.

> The main speaker (a senior member of the then, Department for Education and Employment {DFEE}) said, 'Inclusion is not about a place but about a setting where we are able to fulfil the children's potential to become a citizen'. The speaker claimed that knowledge would dispel fear. Two teachers in the audience came back at this saying that EBD children affect every pupil they come into contact with. [...] Another teacher spoke and said that 'training is needed, not just educational or practical, but environmental too. "Mainstream" children don't always want to open doors for disabled students, and they don't always take SEN children into consideration.' By this time the speaker was becoming a little agitated as it was becoming clear that the teachers in the room had expected something from this sem-inar in the way of help, but seemed to feel they were getting little more than snap shot examples of less than difficult cases. [...] One teacher said how the teacher has to provide evidence to 'exclude' children which can take a long time and in the mean time affecting all around. [...] There is a conflict between the teachers' demands, and one teacher spoke out and added, 'that on top of all this pressure you have the parents sticking their oar in'.
>
> (Field notes, 2000)

This session alone gave me an insight to a group of teachers who were frustrated with their situation within the mainstream classroom and were venting their anger towards a member of the DfEE, due to their frustrations about difficulties in their place of work. In terms of access to other parents, the Afasic parents' conference (a UK charity which sup-ports children and young people with speech, language and communi-cation impairments and their parents and carers) in April 2001 and a parents evening, run jointly by an LEA and a charity for supporting parents of children identified with SEN, in February 2002 is where I gained the most participants.

## Doing the 'right' thing: ethical implications

I was guided in my research by the British Sociological Association's (BSA's) ethical guidelines. However, I also recognise that there may be tensions between professional bodies of ethics models such as the BSA and theoretical and feminist approaches to ethics (Edwards and Mauthner, 2002). I agree that feminist theory can inform ethical research. The stories I have been told were personal, private and sensitive windows into the tellers' lives. In this research there were some occasions where anonymity was impossible: those involving my daughter. I have talked to her about this research and her inclusion (which she agreed to), and I do not apologise for the lack of anonymity here because unlike children in general, many of whom become 'able' adults, she, like many of the participants' children, will never be able to 'tell' her story via this particular medium.

There were also the ethical implications of truth – whose truth, whose knowledge? This research is based on 24 parents who are the main or predominant carers of an impaired child. This is about their truths based upon their personal experiences. My role in constructing their stories is an active and particular one and I am very aware that 'recognition of the researcher's role on constructing "knowledge" about women [or men] has generated numerous debates about the ethics of "representing the other"' (Gillies and Alldred, 2002: 39). Returning to Wright Mills (1959) and the 'Sociological Imagination', this book focuses on the private and personal troubles of parents who discover their child has an impairment. These intimate narratives form the sociological backbone of this research, and the 'sociological imagination' aids the sociological thinking about the public issues that the social world faces when talking about impairment, disability and exclusion more generally.

## A biographical reflection

In my case, my daughter, born in 1986, was diagnosed with a rare syndrome that the health professionals knew little about. I was only 18 years old and did not understand much of what was going on. I certainly did not think about her education, nor did it occur to me that the syndrome would have an effect on her learning ability, and actually no one told me any differently. She did in fact seem to develop within the 'normal' range (but below average) at all the early developmental stages. However, by the time she reached school age (five years old) her educational attainment was increasingly delayed. I found this very difficult to deal with and consistently denied the severity of her learning disability. However, for me, there was a point when it became difficult to deny, and at that point (certainly by the mid 1990s), and as a single mother I began *the fight*: the fight for mainstream school, home schooling, no school and special school! I really did not know what I wanted, or indeed what was the most appropriate way forward for my daughter. What I did know was that however consuming 'the work' became (visiting professionals, reading books, paying for private consultations, carrying out extra homework and, of course, mothering), I continued; what else I was supposed to do?

## Organisation of the book

In focusing on the experiences of parents of children with impairments this research therefore fills an important gap in understanding all the above issues. By giving voice to parents, I highlight specific problem areas in current debates around education policy and provisions for impaired children identified with SEN. It is within these debates that I draw out the ambiguous and liminal spaces participants in this research inhabit when negotiating their private and public, dependent and independent and (dis)abled worlds.

Chapter 2 lays down the theoretical framework based on 'natural' mothering within the empirical and the cultural and political spheres. It engages with literature, empirical work and theoretical constructions of mothering, inclusion/exclusion, inclusive education and disability. It also begins the engagement with social theory in looking at exclusion, denial and disappointment.

Chapter 3 introduces how mothers or fathers are affected when their child is identified or diagnosed with an impairment. It suggests that although the parents are disappointed that no 'celebration' takes place (if the identification takes place early on) or are shocked and disappointed at the loss of their now-impaired child's future, they still have the capacity to fight for their child in the best way they can. This chapter illustrates some of the tension of dealing with this difficulty, alongside the emotional impact of actually being told, discovering or 'feeling that something is not quite right' with their baby or child. The stories here highlight the emotional roller coaster that parents experience, including denial, feelings of shock, grief, loss (of future, of the 'imagined child', of the assumed 'normal' celebration of the birth and mothering process), disappointment and relief. It does not suggest that the emotional impact on discovery of an impairment is a linear process whereby the above feelings happen and trigger the next one in a predictable order. Rather, it shows that these feelings can surface sporadically and in a messy and unpredictable way. Feelings of shock, disappointment, loss and grief in the early stages of a diagnosis are often compounded with feelings of anxiety brought on by difficulties in dealing with the unknown.

Chapter 4 highlights how pivotal the identification and assessment process is in relation to how parents negotiate and become part of the process of 'special' education and support services. While the mothers and fathers may have come into contact with health and social work professionals prior to this assessment process, the statutory assessment and statementing process sees a growth of professional involvement. It is here that there seems to be a point of conflict between the parents and the professionals. However, I am under no illusion that the professionals are the 'baddies' and the parents are 'victims'. I unpack the parents' stories in relation to New Labour policies and directives, especially with regard to professional/parental partnerships and inclusion and anti-exclusionary discourses (followed up in Chapter 5). I illustrate how the parents I interviewed struggle with their own desire to have a child without impairment, and in addition, have a strong desire to take care of and fight for their impaired child, and yet still need the support and help of special education or health services. This chapter shows that the official process is not set up *for* the parents, but 'includes' the parents. This process includes education providers (mainly schools), LEAs, health and social work professionals and policies and directives. This means that relationships between them are often fraught with conflict and difficulty. Parents enter this process with certain expectations often fuelled by emotions and desire, whereas the professionals enter from the position of an 'employee'.

The main arguments in Chapter 5 illustrate how the parents experience 'special' education, whether in mainstream schools or in other types of special units or special schools. This chapter also suggests that inclusive education policies and directives are in direct conflict with the testing and examination culture in the current mainstream environment. These policies deny that there are practical difficulties to parenting children with impairment, which then affect the management of the education process. In a way, the arguments that permeate inclusive education pale into insignificance in the light of what the parents in this research have to say about their special education experience. However, these conflicts about inclusive education directly affect parents' emotional and practical lives. Furthermore, this chapter highlights some of the difficulties in negotiating lived experiences of impairment and disability, both in relation to the parents' own preconceived prejudices about special education provision and other mothers' negative attitudes towards 'difficult' behaviour within a mainstream environment. Ultimately, though, this chapter reveals that these arguments are not simply about inclusive education and exclusion, but about acceptance of difference and difficulty.

Chapter 6 shows that a family with an impaired child is, in fact, in some ways 'disabled'. Support networks are often strained. A mother's or father's mental health can be dramatically affected, leading to depression and anxiety and treatment with anti-depressants and beta-blockers. This has an effect not only on the individual, but on the family, on relationships between parents and their other children and on medical and health professionals. This chapter highlights the fact that the main carer often has to maintain longer periods of responsibilities in the home, and the role of the mother often changes into that of multi-functional 'professional parent' – of social worker, advocate, carer and nurse – which then impacts on the mother's potential career path. Furthermore, it indicates that the mother may choose to work outside the home, not only for financial gain but also for respite. Chapter 6 also reveals that a parent can become isolated in a world where she or he has already compromised a large part of her or his potential working life and feels unable to break free from it. This is experienced both emotionally and practically, as others' reactions to her or his impaired child result in a withdrawal from mainstream public places, as well as imposed exclusions from others.

Chapter 7 concludes the book by returning to the concepts; exclusion, denial and disappointment, theoretically in discovering difference and experiencing difficulty. It poses questions and statements about the social, political and cultural spheres in parenting children with impairments in moving ideas forward.

# 2
# Mothering and Disability: The Social, Cultural and Political Spheres

> Whereas the family might once have been responsible for creating – bringing up – what we might call a whole citizen, it is now primarily responsible for the vital period of early socialisation, up until the age of four or five, when the state begins to take over through the education system. As this period of early socialisation becomes more specialised, so it too becomes a form of professional activity. [...] What might be disappearing is the idea of bringing up children as a normal part of life, with all its messiness and contradictions, pleasures, satisfactions *and* deprivations [emphasis in original].
>
> (Craib, 1994: 84)

Ian Craib highlights the messiness of 'normal' family practices in late modern society in an attempt to suggest that increased expectations, individualism and the intrusion of 'experts' have contributed to feelings of disappointment with one's lot. In this chapter I introduce the reader to what becoming a mother is via cultural, political and social spheres, theoretically. All contribute to how mothers and fathers consider and experience their life course. Culturally, high expectations are abundant in view of the privileging of the 'normal', socially appropriate, aesthetically desirable and intellectually able, in childrearing and family practice. Political discourses on inclusive education, and partnership too, infer that difference is to be celebrated and embraced. Theoretical concepts aid me to frame an analysis in thinking through these experienced and abstract sociological issues. This chapter addresses these statements in introducing mothering and learning 'disability'.

21

## 'Natural' mothering

The field of literature within family studies, social theory, sociology and social psychology undeniably suggests that parenting a child within late modern society, in general, can be a challenging, risky and turbulent task (Miller, 2005; Morgan, 1996; Ribbens, 1994). Also suggested is that expectations associated with childbirth and childrearing, perfection and normality, based on changing notions of what it is to be a mother or father and a human being, can often be shattered by real-life experiences (Beck and Beck-Gernsheim, 1995; Craib, 1994). Families who have a child or children with some kind of impairment may, therefore, be faced with challenges that go beyond any expectation (see Beresford, 1995; Gray, 2002 and Read, 2000 for families with children with severe, attention, sensory and/or physical impairments).

Psychologically, Winnicot (1988) argues that the mother spends her time during pregnancy preparing for the changes ahead, as does the father in a different capacity. However, many parents who have financial, relationship and health problems, for example, may rarely experience 'natural', 'ordinary' or 'normal' parenting (Smart, 1996; Walbank, 2001). Preparing for motherhood and fatherhood does not necessarily prepare any prospective parent for a difficult or impaired child. The romanticised notion of perfect children and 'good enough' mothering does not indicate that the birth may be horrible, the baby inconsolable, terminally ill or impaired. Significantly, there has been research that indicates there is 'considerable amount of sympathy with the parents and doctors involved in cases where [impaired] babies are allowed to die' (Chadwick, 1987: 93).

Men and women may decide to have children based on romantic notions 'closely linked with the emotional needs of the parents' (Beck and Beck-Gernsheim, 1995: 105) and a desire to see 'oneself embodied in the next generation and represented again in human form' (Hurrelmann in ibid.). These romantic expectations as well as an expectation to have a 'normal' baby can only increase the likelihood of dashed hopes and the disappointment of parents who discover their baby or child has impairments. Even deeper into the psyche, the idea of reproducing one's self in a child who is subsequently impaired may impact emotionally and psychologically at a level that goes beyond our discursive understanding. Expectations of childrearing, though, are often linked to what parents read or hear about from professionals, popular literature and the media.

At an advisory level, mothers and fathers often take on board professional and practical advice written in books and magazines. Countless debates on whether the mother, and indeed the father, should or should not be practically and emotionally involved in childrearing have emerged over the decades. There have been the authoritarian, emotionless rules in the mother-care manuals of the 1920s and 30s like Liddiard's (1954) *The Mothercraft Manual*, or the permissive, emotional and 'instinctual loving' written about in Spock's (1946[1973]) *Baby and Childcare*, as in the 1940s and 50s. Then, in the 1970s and 80s, a different manual was produced, a more 'fun' version of childrearing. Miriam Stoppard (1984) wrote *The Babycare Book*, which positioned the father in the picture, promoting equal care from both parents. Stoppard (1985) has also written - *Pregnancy and Birth Handbook*, which has been revised throughout the 1990s due to its popularity and updated medical advice. There is little to prepare the mother for impairment in this literature, and ideas about 'ordinary mothering' and feeling 'natural' about the whole process remain explicit and implicit in the text.

If there is a mention of impairment or abnormalities it is often in relation to Down's syndrome and tests that highlight certain impairments with a view to either keeping the baby or terminating the pregnancy, based on amniocentesis test results (Stoppard, 1985). Problematically, Winnicot (1964, 1988) explains that being an 'ordinary mother' is 'natural' and that others should not interfere in this process for fear of damaging what can only be described as a complete and harmonious union. 'When a mother has a capacity quite simply to be a mother we must never interfere' (ibid., 1988: 13). However, very often parents who discover their child has impairments will seek and desire this professional 'interference' and expertise as a means to diagnose and support.

Moore (1996: 58) argues, 'Mothering and motherhood are not, contrary to popular belief, "the most natural things in the world"'. The 'motherhood myth', according to Forna (1998: 3) is that of perfection, as it suggests the mother must be devoted to her child and her role in every way. She must be all loving, giving and able to understand her child's every need. Forna's (ibid.: 5) examples of a woman who preferred to say she was infertile rather than to admit that she simply did not choose motherhood, and of another mother who, while cherishing her children, regretted her decision to become a mother, are indicative of how social pressures are felt by women regarding motherhood. Mothering, according to Coward (1997: 118),

demands changes in your life and it changes you, sometimes unleashing feelings that can quite easily drive you crazy. Women can find themselves up against unexpected emotions of anger and gnawing guilt, instead of living up to the idealised version of goodness poured out to good children.

Mothers who have impaired children are doubly damned (in the above sense) when they have children who behave, or simply are, outside of the norm. Not only do the mothers in my research have to take on board all of these social pressures regarding norms of motherhood and childrearing, but also experience the practical difficulty of mothering a child with impairment.

Benn (1998), Forna (1998) and Richardson (1993), all stress the guilt a mother can face in relation to 'ordinary' mothering. Forna (1998: 12), simply but forcefully, says:

> Guilt has become so strongly associated with motherhood that it is often considered to be a natural emotion. [...] Guilt is *not* a biological hormonally-driven response. Women feel guilty because they are made to. Mothers are told that every failure, every neglected talk, every dereliction of their growing duties, every refusal to sacrifice will be seared upon their child's psyche, will mar his or her future, and damage not only the mother–child relationship but every subsequent relationship in the child's life. That is, if the mother who is found to be wanting doesn't create a juvenile delinquent or a fully-fledged criminal [emphasis in original].

In this literature it seems that if the mother is not seen to be proactive in her child's welfare before and after the birth, and if something goes 'wrong', then the mother is often blamed. In talking about impairment and parenting, Avery's (1999: 119) response to guilt suggests 'a deep parental investment in our culture's conflated ideologies in the areas of "good" parenting and "perfect" children. It seems clear that we parents tend to situate our children's disability as personal punishment'. In the following chapters though, guilt is not one of the main emotions experienced, and parents do not see their child's impairment as their fault or, indeed, as a personal punishment. Guilt is often experienced as a reflexive response to how one might have behaved or thought in a momentary or past situation. More important, though, is not the guilt but the disappointment in relation to what was expected from the 'normal' mothering process.

Wallbank (2001: 6–7) examines Foucault's conceptualisation of normalisation in relation to different theories of motherhood and, specifically, lone motherhood. Simplified, normalisation is a process by which individuals have to conform to norms and are in turn judged and measured on how closely they get to conform to the desired norm, in this case, mothering. If the individual does not adhere to or falls 'outside of what has been defined and valued as normal' then he or she may be 'marginalized and is in need of modification'. According to Foucault (1977), in an attempt to conform to the norm, which is the ultimate goal, surveillance of the self becomes apparent. A gaze becomes internalised in some way and results in a powerful self-discipline.

Wallbank's ideas can be linked not only to lone parenting but also to the perpetuation of normal parenting in relation to impaired children. General ideas of what it is to be a good mother are embodied in the policies and definitions of a particular time. Smart (1996: 46) runs through various good and bad practices that are historically and culturally specific and changing, for example, breast- or hygienically prepared bottle milk, good and bad practices about where the baby might sleep, and whether the baby sleeps on its back, which was bad in the 1970s and 80s but good from the 1990s. All of these aspects of normalising mothering contain within them presumptions about love and devotion for the child. But even the demonstration of love has changed over time. Spensky, in Smart (1996: 46–7), shows that 'for some mothers their love was thought to be best expressed by giving up their babies for adoption so that better-placed, married couples could raise them "properly". By the 1970s, however, this mother-love was best expressed by wishing to keep such an illegitimate child'. Mothers, specifically of children with impairments, do have to negotiate this normalisation process and are constantly calling into question their notions of good mothering initiated from their own emotional acceptance of the impairment and that of other's presumptions about how to parent in general.

Richardson (1993: 4) suggests that mothers often blame themselves for feeling unhappy and depressed about their position as a mother and this in turn reflects their mothering abilities because they may then also take these feelings out on the child in frustration. The 'good' mother is supposed to sacrifice the self in order to nurture the child's new life. However, Read (2000: 10) argues that 'parents were *assumed* to feel guilty for having a disabled child and the guilt was further alleged to be a force that drove their actions and lifestyles in ways too innumerable to count' [emphasis added]. Significantly, a 'baby book' left in many hospitals suggests, 'Don't worry if you don't feel a great surge of maternal love all at once; it's all there waiting to develop' (Richardson, 1993: 54). There are some mothers of children with and without impairments who never 'feel bonded' with their child and yet still maintain 'good enough' mothering.

However, in research on mothers and childrearing in general, Ribbens (1994) found that 'a third of her respondents actually indicated that to resort to outside advice was somehow an admission of failure to cope with something that they should have been able to manage themselves' (ibid.: 75). Reiterated here, Craib (1994: 86) suggests 'as the family's early socialisation functions become marginalised' school and friendship networks have taken on a greater importance and this is where conflict can arise for both families with an impaired child and those without, due to a withdrawal of the parents' autonomous power over their child's future. Furthermore, families who have a child with impairments often find it difficult to maintain a wholly private sphere based on a child's, sometimes, socially inappropriate behaviour (Gray, 2002), physical appearance (Maes et al., 2003) and professional intervention (Cole, 2004; Read, 2000).

Ideas about who is responsible for the child and family are crucial within this research. Both Rose (1989) and Donzelot (1979) suggest that historically there has been an increased shift towards the involvement of the state and professional 'expert' in the running of families. The family then becomes a site of surveillance, placing increased pressure on the parents, and more often on the mother, to produce 'normal' children. If there were problems with specific childrearing practices,

> norms of adjustment and maladjustment would be produced and refined, and normalisation would be undertaken. Norms of adjustment, practices likely to produce adjustment, and visions of maladjustment would be disseminated from the clinics back into the institutional and family life.
>
> (Rose, 1989: 158)

For example, currently in England and Wales, the Statement of SEN (record of needs in Scotland) that is produced when a child presents with difficulties in learning specifies and legitimises certain intrusions by education and health professionals. However, because the desire to produce a well-adjusted 'normal' child is so great, and because of their own emotional responses and insecurities in discovering their child has impairments and/or difficulties, parents, as I have said, often want this 'intrusion' into the private life of the family.

The desire to be a good mother and care for her family run alongside the desire to have children as an experience related to an 'extended self' (Beck and Beck-Gernsheim, 1995: 105). Mothers see their children as either moving towards independence, autonomy and separateness or again as 'extensions of themselves; to be told what to do until they left home'

(Smart and Neale, 1999: 106). The impaired child's position is in conflict with these parental expectations, for example, a child on the autistic spectrum and unable to communicate cannot be an extension of the mother's self without her angst about what that self is. Or a child with an intellectual impairment may be unable to negotiate full independence, autonomy or separateness and therefore challenge a mother or father's notion of being a parent in successfully rearing a fully independent young adult. This certain kind of loss (that of the 'normal' child's future, for example) can be unpacked within sociological theory used by both Craib (1994) and Cohen (2001) (discussed in more detail later on in the chapter).

These deep-seated emotions are often what lie at the heart of mothers and fathers when faced with an impaired child, as indicated by Read (2000).

> Mothers often believe that they have knowledge, perspectives and insights of which others need to be convinced. That insight is gained through their close involvement with the child and through their own knowledge of what life offers on the other side of the track. They often have the conviction that others who have not been there do not know what it is like and also that in many respects, it is not something of much significance to them.
>
> (2000: 120)

Not only are these dilemmas associated with mothers in Britain, but in other Western countries also. For example, in thinking more specifically about experiencing difficulty and impairment, Gray (2002) found that Australian families of children with high functioning autism experienced different types of negative stigma. The following section takes the context of mothering and impairment further.

## Mothering in context

While mothering and the family lie at the heart of this book, debates and discourses on inclusion and exclusion and on children identified with SEN within wider sociological debates are crucial. Namely, because inclusionary policies across the board hide implicit exclusionary tactics and experiences, and in addition these debates can cut across disability, class, unemployment, gender, behaviour and ethnicity alike. Generally, the works of Lister (1998) and Levitas (1998, 2001) have emphasised the link between paid work, education and inclusionary policies. Levitas (2001: 451) identifies a parallel between exclusionary and underclass debates, *including* the 'unemployable'. This is important on two accounts here.

1. For the mothers and fathers who cannot work due to their 'caring' commitments
2. The potential employability or (non employability) of their impaired child

This is increased by Gordon Brown's new deal for 'making work pay', which targets lone parents, long-term unemployed and those people with impairments. These debates impact upon this research in the following ways:

- The impaired unemployed are marginalised or excluded from being full citizens based on their unemployed/poor status. This affects parents' expectations of the future of their child/young adult (see Chapter 3).
- Inclusionary debates directly impact upon special education and disability policies, even though current mainstream education sites may not always be the most appropriate place to educate all impaired children (see Chapters 4 and 5).
- The main carer of an impaired child may have to 'drop out' of paid employment because of the responsibilities and demands of their unpaid care work, leaving them excluded from the 'worthy workforce' (see Chapter 6).
- The main carer may experience exclusion via others' pre-conceived perceptions of disability, difference and difficulty (see Chapters 5 and 6).

These debates are not exclusive to public policy and can be discussed at a deeper, culturally and historically defined level. Sibley (1995: 51), a geographer, plays a part in these debates by unpacking the 'imperfect' and 'grotesque' in relation to exclusion, and suggests, '[t]he idea of society assumes some cohesion and conformity which create, and are threatened by, difference, although what constitutes a threatening difference has varied considerably over time and space' (ibid.: 69). However, even in late modernity it seems that an aversion to the 'grotesque' and mentally impaired has not changed dramatically as indicated by Chadwick (1987: 110) in her discussion about problematic reproductive technologies and the 'elimination of genetic defects [...] suggesting that the handicapped [*sic*] have less right to live'.

# Being human?

This aversion to the 'grotesque' and 'vile' is an old theme in Western thought, and one explored by Jonathan Swift (1967 [1726]). *Gulliver's Travels* engages with ideas about denigration of the human form, mental ability, social norms and rationality to the point of being disgusted by human beings per se. It culminates in the final book where he discovers a breed of humans (Yahoos) who display no social graces and are unable to communicate with language. He wanted to disassociate himself from them and befriend the horse creatures (Houyhnhnms) that were graceful and could communicate at a high level. On his return home, he despises the human beings that he is closest to in form, actually his wife and children, and says, 'but I must freely confess the sight of them filled me only with hatred, disgust and contempt, and the more by reflecting on the near alliance I had to them' (ibid.: 338).

Gulliver finds it difficult to tolerate the sight of the humans, and Swift does not simply play with the idea of eugenics: *Gulliver's Travels* is written through the voice of Gulliver. 'And when I began to consider, that by copulation with one of the Yahoo species, I had become a parent of more, it struck me with the utmost shame, confusion and horror' (ibid.: 339). This clearly taps into notions of thinking psychically about what it is to bring into the world, to create a human being that is not acceptable to the parent and who acts outside the expected and accepted norms  - behaviourally, culturally or intellectually. These ideas can also be seen in Shelley's (1994 [1818]) *Frankenstein*, in which an enthusiastic student creates a being that invokes fear in all those he meets, which leads to tragic and painful consequences.

On a less extreme level, Gulliver, in Swift (1967 [1726]), calls into question his desire to be human, to be in the same room as his wife and children, let alone eat at the same table as they did. Why? Because their habits were disgusting to him; they were too much like the Yahoos, who were dirty, primitive creatures. Clearly, it can be argued that with this aversion to the 'untamed', 'impure' (Douglas, 1966) and the 'dangerous' (Young, 1999), these themes are important in relation to *others'* reactions to the impaired and anti-social, and even debates on exclusion (see also Chapter 5). This can be due to 'anti-social' behaviour such as dribbling, headbanging and screaming, for example.

Shakespeare (1994: 283) considers that much of 'sociological renderings gloss over aspects of normality, conformity and difference, and focus instead on the performative aspects of impairment', whereas his work does an exposé on the cultural representations and imagery of what impairment is seen as. By looking at images and characters in literature, both current and historical, he finds that fear and objectification are key aspects of how disability is perceived, and this is paralleled by the way women and ethnic minorities have been treated within Western culture. He goes on to suggest that it is not the disability but the impairment that causes fear in the able-bodied: 'it is non-disabled people's embodiment which is the issue: disabled people remind non-disabled people of their own vulnerability' (ibid.: 297). Thus, within the cultural sphere it seems there is an aversion to difficult difference. However, this is played out *within* the political sphere, as discussed below, and is implicitly wrapped up in inclusive education discourse.

## 'Inclusive' education and exclusion

In the UK, the late 20th and early 21st centuries have seen an increased promotion of inclusive education, that is, the inclusion of *all* children in mainstream schools *where possible*, including those with impairments. Thinking more specifically about inclusive education, parents' expectations of mainstream education can have a negative impact when their impaired child is unable to access it or when the child is unable to maintain his or her education within the 'chosen' mainstream school. 'Inclusion' within mainstream education is implemented by the current government and promoted as an anti-exclusionary policy. However, current research is already indicating that actual inclusion (the child *experiencing* inclusion as well as being placed in a mainstream environment) is not necessarily occurring in practice (Allan, 1999; Benjamin, 2002). Furthermore, if provision and policies are based on one element of need then children's individual difficulties, and therefore needs (social as well as educational), may not be met. It could be argued, therefore, that inclusive education is not a policy or a directive, but is rhetoric based on ideals about promoting tolerance of difference. Such rhetoric ignores the experience of parenting a child identified with additional learning needs both in relation to their general and social education.

Inclusive education would ideally be promoted if the structures to implement a differentiated, and yet integrative, education were in place (Norwich, 2000). Norwich believes that exclusion of children with SEN in mainstream education is not acceptable and yet neither is the promotion of choice that gives the LEAs, the schools and the parents enough room to exclude a child on the basis of a particular disability or need. This promotion of choice is often seen as a way of exercising 'preferences for teaching programmes' (ibid.: 24–25), but was also pushed by the British Conservative government of the 1980s and 90s. Importantly though, the child, the family and the educators should be at the centre of this debate, rather than the education centre, beaconed as an inclusionary option. As it stands currently, the conflict is between a desire to embrace difference based on a philosophy of equal rights and prioritising educational performance structuring it in such a way that it leaves little room for difference and creativity due to the highly structured testing and examination culture (Rogers, 2007).

A Foucauldian analysis of mainstream pupils in a classroom situation of children identified with SEN sees the mainstream pupils setting up their own discourses around how to work and behave alongside the children with SEN.

> This had its own set of rules and features such as pastoral power and pedagogic strategies, and its effect was simultaneously to regulate and disrupt their conduct towards pupils with special needs. The mainstream pupils' governmental regime was broadly positive and supportive of pupils with special needs, but at times was highly punitive, legitimising the exclusion of individuals.
>
> (Allan, 1999: 3)

Such behaviour could be said to legitimise official power based on what may be viewed as positive moves towards inclusion. Yet at the same time this power is being exercised over children with SEN, therefore increasing their experiences of marginalisation and exclusion, and thus compounding any sense of worthlessness and subordination. Benjamin (2002: 129–130), on inclusive education in a girls' mainstream comprehensive reveals,

> I manage to spend most of the lesson working with Cassandra, although I do spend some time with the other students. Most of the work is beyond them. I'm sure inclusive education is not supposed to mean everyone being given the opportunity to do the same work, irrespective of whether they can learn from it. I'm feeling irritated by a morning spent trying to 'make the curriculum accessible' when it manifestly isn't.

Neither of these quotes seem to suggest that inclusive education is working, but if it is true that by virtue of inclusion the British educational system promotes a tolerance of difference, then surely this is a positive move forward. However, negatively, tolerance does rather imply to 'put up with'.

Perhaps it would be useful to consider whether exclusion within inclusive education is more damaging than a different education site. Gray (2002: 745) in his study of 'felt and enacted stigma' highlights these points regarding mainstream school with regard to children who have high functioning autism or AS. He reveals that parents often have difficulties in negotiating the education process. One of his participants said,

> I've had a gut-full. Just ... school last week. I thought, I've had a gut-full of this. Why am I bothering? Why am I pushing him through school? Why don't I take him out? Give him distance education'. I'm sick of the hassles with school.

Wilson (1999: 110) suggests that we take a step back from the ideological rhetoric of inclusion and concentrate on the aims of identifying the best possible way to educate, within an environment that encourages individual skills. He puts forward the argument that not all of us want to be academics or great sports people, but this should not exclude us from having an inclusive community and social activities.

> The clash between these two perspectives is that including everybody within the same group seems inconsistent with fulfilling a particular group's purpose. We *want* competent musicians, good cricketers, excellent mathematicians and so on. More than this: if I am unable to play a musical instrument at all, it seems to make little sense to say that I can be included in an orchestra which is to play Beethoven or if I cannot even add up or subtract that I should be in a group learning quadratic equations. Of course, I can just sit there in the same place alongside others but this is hardly inclusion in any serious sense. But then, it could be argued, I ought not to be 'left out' of these activities, however incompetent I am. If any and every activity has its particular purpose and criteria of competence to which, through no fault of my own, I cannot measure up, how can this be done? [emphasis in original].

Whatever we do can be equally valued, but this does not seem to be enough with regard to the notion of inclusion. Difference is not privileged in the way that it could be. If there were not such negative attitudes towards different place, different child and different needs, maybe there would be less prejudice with regard to SEN and disability in general. Of course, the conflict between raising British educational standards and inclusion means that it is constantly a battle between churning out 'excellent' pupils and meeting the needs of children with difficulties. A discourse of acceptance is almost impossible if excellence in academic ability is always privileged. However, if all schools were considered as inclusive education centres, meeting the needs of different children within different criteria would be the way forward. Furthermore, rather than place the emphasis on inclusion, education centres would be seen as places to educate and that would mean a need for collaboration between various centres (mainstream, special and otherwise), in order to provide a whole educational approach while meeting the needs of each child. Any collaboration need not be at the local level, whereby the pupil experiences an eclectic education, but at the planning stage within training programmes, structure and public policy.

Allan (1999) has found an obvious discourse on 'normality' within mainstream education, which shapes the experiences of both children with SEN and those without: many of the pupils without SEN either tolerated or excluded these children. Her research did not, however, address the deeper contradictions that lie at the heart of these experiences such as cultural adversity towards difference, and her focus was mainly on the children's experiences. Moreover, although studies have shown that parents have been drawn into the debate, public policy has accentuated tensions between individual rights and interests, and collective justice and equity (Norwich, 2000; Simmons, 2000). This has caused a divide among common interest groups (parents of children with SEN), between parents who want children to be included in mainstream education and to fit into society, and parents who believe that inclusive education only exacerbates the problems the child faces socially, culturally and educationally.

According to Riddell (2000: 109), disability rights literature suggests there are different types of parents and choices.

> The choices of radical parents (that is, those wishing the system to become more clearly inclusive) are seen as legitimate, but parents supporting a separate special system of education, apart from parents of deaf children, would be seen as profoundly misguided and therefore ignored.

Although important, I suggest that these debates are divisive. Inclusive policies and disability rights discourses can feed into negative assumptions about special schools for example, and therefore potentially set parents up for disappointment if mainstream education does not work for their child.

For example, Oliver (1996: 94), in his discussion on 'education for all', suggests that the 'twenty-first century will see the struggle of disabled people for inclusion go from strength to strength. In such a struggle, special, segregated education has no role to play'. However, specifically for children with learning impairments and EBD there are additional educational and social criteria to consider.

## Experiencing disability

Disability rights and inclusive education debates suggest that a disabled child included within mainstream education will be marginalised and ridiculed (Rioux, 1999), *or* those children who are not included within mainstream education are discriminated against (Armstrong et al., 2000). However, positive debates about special schools or special units for the education of learning disabled children are not about accepting that those children are uneducable, but that difference and difficulty is realised and accepted, not implicitly denied or embellished in inclusive discourses.

There are many positions on what it means to be included both at a political and experiential level (Oliver, 1996; Shakespeare, 1994; Vincent, 2000). However, as I understand 'becoming disabled', it is not purely about the imposition of an impairment that happens to a human being when suddenly struck down by disease or caught up in a 'tragic' accident. But that discourses on 'becoming disabled' are paralleled with stories about exclusion, stigmatisation, isolation and prejudice when a parent discovers she or he has an impaired children. There are two spheres of this experience: a macro sphere (which includes the political and the cultural), where disabilism is imposed upon the family or individual, based on the impairment; and a micro sphere (which includes the cultural and the experiential), where experiences are felt privately and internally as an emotional response to *becoming* a parent of an impaired child. Therefore these parental stories are not well defined; in neither *being* nor *becoming* physically or learning disabled, but neither do they live *without* impairment.

Avery (1999) and Gray (2002) in their research on parents with impaired children use Goffman (1963) to unpack what he defined as 'courtesy stigma'. That is 'a phenomena of the gaze that not only judges the differently embodied Other, but endows entire families with the stigma of disability ...' (Avery, 1999: 117). Gray (2002) discusses enacted and felt stigma experienced by Australian parents of children with high functioning autism or AS. Enacted stigma, according to Gray, is the reaction of others when faced with a child who behaves outside of expected norms. Felt stigma is associated with a perceived notion of stigma, for example, an internal feeling of embarrassment, shame or inadequacy. These terms have been useful when conceptualising the two themes that straddle my research: the disabilism and prejudice that are imposed upon the family by society and the internal and personal experiences of the family via the narratives of either the mother or father.

I would suggest that Slack (1999: 29–30) describes her experience here of moving into the world of disability as 'felt stigma'.

> The transition into a wheelchair user from a physical education teacher who thrived on space and freedom and movement was not easy. For a start no one told me what I should do with all this store of anger which grew into volcanic proportions inside of me. I was so frightened of all that anger. How could such volume be contained safely inside one body and never seep to escape causing unsuspecting harm? Just like the nuclear reactors scattered across our world. Such power has to go somewhere – doesn't it? [...] I communicated with the world and myself through the medium of perpetual motion. It was who I was.

Slack, like some of the parents who took part in this research, was frightened by, if not unable to always deal with, the intensity of feeling produced by experiencing disability first hand, (or via courtesy stigma in the case of parents in this research). Morris (1991: 17) sustained a paralysing injury after falling off a wall to help a child in need. She writes about her own experiences of prejudice as well as those of others she has researched, and regarding disabilism and prejudice she says here:

> It is not normal to have a difficulty walking or to be unable to walk: it is not normal to be unable to see, to hear; it is not normal to be incontinent, to have fits, to experience extreme tiredness, to be in constant pain; it is not normal to have a limb or limbs missing. If we have a learning disability the way we interact with others usually reveals our difference. These are the types of intellectual and physical characteristics which distinguish our experience from that of the majority of the population. They are all part of the human experience but they are not the norm ...

It is to springboard from all this messiness related to experiencing impairment and disability that leads me into the theoretical framework that straddles the cultural, political and experiential.

## Introducing the conceptual: exclusion, denial and disappointment

Stanley Cohen (2001), Ian Craib (1994) and Jock Young (1999) all address the *experiential difficulties* of living in contemporary society. This is why they are important in the analysis of mothering and disability. In this section I parallel some of their theorisations in relation to disappointment, denial and social exclusion/inclusion and parents with impaired children. As a psychotherapist and professor of sociology, Craib (1994) uses social theory as well as psychoanalytic theory in his thesis on disappointment. Cohen (2001) too uses psychoanalytic theory as a tool in his thesis on denial, but is mainly influenced by the sociologist Goffman (1963, 1969) and criminological theory. Young (1999) draws on social and criminological theory in his thesis on social exclusion. I expand upon all of these below and throughout the book. Even though Craib and Cohen have been influenced by psychoanalysis, my use of their theories is sociological and not psychoanalytic in its analysis.

To begin then, Young (1999) suggests that in late modern society there is a belief that diversity and difference are accepted and even celebrated, and that social structures are in place to incorporate differences, for example, policies on inclusion and, arguably, inclusive education. Positive assumptions about diverse family patterns, inclusive education, academic excellence, parental/professional partnerships and the work–home life balance, as well as simply accepting difference, seem part and parcel of contemporary life. Young (1999: 59) says late modern societies '*consume* diversity' and 'do not recoil at difference', and yet '[w]hat they are less willing to endure is *difficulty*' [emphasis in original]. He goes on to claim that

> [t]he late modern world celebrates diversity and *difference*, which it readily absorbs and sanitizes; what it cannot abide is difficult people and *dangerous* classes, which it seeks to build the most elaborate defences against, not just in terms of insiders and outsiders, but throughout the population [emphasis in original].
>
> (ibid.)

Young relates much of his work to criminality and deviance, but the parents in my research within their world of impairment and disability can be seen as paralleling the 'difficult' people and 'dangerous' classes. This is highlighted specifically with regard to assumptions about the celebration of difference alongside the defences against difficult people.

In the main, mothers who have impaired children would be both different and difficult for the education system and any family unit. Inclusive policies suggest that Young (1999) is correct in his assumption about celebrating difference. Yet this 'celebration' of difference is not translated into social practice, as the parental narratives show. Children with impairments may move in and out of behaviour that is considered vulgar, distasteful or, simply, socially inappropriate. This, in many ways, cannot be sanitised, and therefore slips from being different into being difficult; as impaired children at school and their families are considered difficult. Cultural and practical exclusionary tactics are implicitly or explicitly used in contradiction to the rhetoric of inclusive policies and the celebration of difference. Furthermore, although Young (1999) suggests that diversity is celebrated, he also suggests that historically it became more and more tolerated, while difficulty became less and less so. As I suggested, my understanding of tolerance is to 'put up with', not celebrate, therefore continuing to imply a negative attitude towards difference. The result of this may be that attitudes and actions become more implicit, but still penetrate deeper levels of cultural attitudes. Moreover, there is a denial of difficulty within policy discourse and those that celebrate difference, which leaves the experiences of parents of impaired children in a liminal space.

This 'celebration of difference' could be understood via Cohen's (2001: 52) work, where '[d]enial and normalization reflect personal and cultural states in which suffering is not acknowledged'. Cohen, within a broad human rights and sociological frame, discusses human rights violations and mass atrocities in analysing denial. My interest in this book lies in where he draws out different types of denial, which cause difficulties for individuals and groups when they face a situation or experience something they may not be comfortable with, as in the case when a parent discovers her or his child has a learning impairment. However, denying difficulty can be beneficial for an individual's mental health. And Cohen (2001: 53) asks, in relation to patients on their discovery of a fatal or serious illness, 'is there a right way to cope with information about traumatic, catastrophic or disabling losses?' Becoming a parent in general can be experienced as challenging in late modern society, and some might even say traumatic. Significantly though, for the parent of an impaired child, living with *additional* difficulties can be intolerable, such as increased visits to doctors and other professionals, a child's anti-social behaviour (e.g., faeces smearing, continual screaming and aggression), fraught social relations and others' reactions to their child.

Denying difficulty or an impairment, at times, may simply be part and parcel of coping and as Cohen (2001: 54) powerfully explains,

[u]nless psychotically cut off from reality, no one is a total denier or non-denier, still less either 'in denial' or 'out of denial' permanently. People give different accounts to themselves and others; elements of partial denial and partial acknowledgement are always present; we oscillate rapidly between states. Families and treatment staff are often exasperated at seeing newly disabled patients fluctuate between awareness and radical denial of their condition. [...] Just when you think that you have finally 'come to terms' with the illness, you realize that this acceptance was truly self-deceptive – a mere internal public relations exercise – and that layers of reality remain unconfronted.

As with parents in this study, it is not simply a matter of either being 'in denial' or 'out of denial'. As the reader discovers in the following chapters parents can be harshly reminded of emotional pain that was once forgotten (or denied) at times throughout their life course.

Denial exists not only within the private experiential sphere, but also within the public political sphere. As with 'denying' mass atrocities (Cohen 2001), denial of a disabled discourse in the 'celebration of difference' and 'inclusive' education policies is highlighted when experiences of inclusion and exclusion are described. By illuminating the contradictions between inclusive education policy and practice and a highly competitive academic environment denial can be observed. Furthermore, parents' narratives compound it.

Denial and exclusion, it could be suggested, are a result of cultural and political expectations. Rightly or wrongly, expectations of a norm, whether they are in the form of a particular physical body, ability, behaviour, family practice, policy or political discourse, are apparent. Particularly, from pregnancy to death, parents have wishes, desires and expectations for their offspring and how they experience this parent–child relationship. On thinking about childrearing, parents imagine what kind of mother or father they will be, whether their baby will be a boy or girl and how their baby will develop. As the child grows, expectations of a certain life are already entrenched.

Generally, desires for a child to gain a good education, get a job, have children or get married are mapped out within the parents' social world. These desires and expectations are challenged, not just at birth but also recurrently. Craib (1994), within a frame of psychoanalytic and social theory, describes the everyday experiences of difficulty and suggests that it is 'normal' to feel disappointment with contemporary life. He does this by drawing on his own experiences and ideas as a psychotherapist and sociologist. He suggests that living in late modern society, especially in Britain and North America, what we might hope for, desire or expect has become less clear. There are consistent unrealistic high expectations of what contemporary life should be like based on individualistic notions. Yet as Craib stresses, we are not in a world of individuals. We cannot help but be involved in social relations and it is within those relations that disappointment occurs. The human condition is such that people consistently feel disappointed with their lot, and this disappointment is necessary in re-evaluating their existence within the social world. Dashed expectations lead individuals to believe they are depressed or unhappy and in need of a cure.

Disappointment is important in my sociological analysis of mothering an impaired child on more than one level. On one level parents experience disappointment when their life is not how they imagined it would be. It is practically difficult and they are at times frustrated and angry. And then, on another level when they 'lose' their 'imagined' child they again feel disappointed for *themselves* and encounter depression or, at least, sadness. This can be described in the case of a mother who has just been informed that her baby has Down's syndrome, or a father who is told his child is on the autistic spectrum. She or he may have any number of emotional responses but the fact is, there is a certain kind of loss, loss of the 'normal' expected child. Then, there is also loss of the 'normal' celebration of that child. Moreover, there is a significant loss bound up with the additional difficulty in dealing with the everyday life of impairment.

> [W]e rage against a world which will not be as we want it to be. The claim 'I have a right to control my own life', when made collectively by a subjugated people, has a very different meaning to that which it has when made by an individual. I spend my life surrounded by other people, who are more or less independent of me and constantly doing things on their own account. As a consequence, I have to adjust to them. If I am to control my own life, then I will first have to control the lives of those around me. The rights I might have to do as I wish are certainly a political matter, but they are also a moral matter.
>
> (Craib, 1994: 7)

Craib argues that there is necessity about feeling loss, grief, disappointment, and indeed misery. However, parents in this research experience, in addition to 'ordinary' disappointment within Western consumer culture and individualism, the experience of a disabled child.

The narratives of parents throughout this book exemplify the social effects on relationships with family members and the outside world. These deep-seated emotions are often what lie at the hearts of mothers and fathers when faced with a child who has impairments. More importantly, late modern discourses gloss over and deny emotional difficulties such as loss, disappointment, and more generally mothering a child with impairments, and concentrate on the educationally and physically able as well as placing all within an inclusive celebratory discourse. This actually ignores and denies the difficulties experienced by many parents of impaired children. This book illustrates that parents, throughout this study, have emotional responses to disappointment, denial and exclusion. Furthermore, these terms are also unpacked regarding the wider social and public responses to difficulty, disappointment, denial and exclusion/inclusion both implicitly and explicitly within policy discourse and public reactions.

## Reflections

This chapter has raised questions about 'natural' mothering within the context of impairment and disability. There is certainly an expectation of the 'normal', if not the imagined perfect birth, baby, child and life course, in becoming a mother and mothering. This is fuelled by popular, cultural and political discourses on what it is to be a mother and mothering practices. By looking at 'normal' mothering and family practices, as dictated by magazines, the media and experts, and at aversions to difficult difference, via stories in literature and empirical studies, the cultural sphere literally screams of high expectations in becoming a mother and negative responses from other individuals towards difference.

In addition, the political sphere, via discourses and policies on inclusive education, and academic competition have not served to obliterate prejudice and discrimination but instead cause conflict between 'disabled groups' and their families in their attempts to gain the most appropriate education for their children. Predominantly, the narratives that come alive within following chapters are about personal experiences of difficulty, disappointment, denial and exclusion. It is from thinking through the questions and statements that have been raised in this chapter about 'natural' mothering, disappointment, denial and exclusion within the cultural and political spheres that impact the experiential sphere. The following chapter unpacks the initial stories in 'discovering difference'.

# 3
# Mothering: Identification and Diagnosis of Impairment

There is a rich stock of folk knowledge and personal and family experience about how people first react to being diagnosed as having a fatal or serious illness and then cope with their condition. For some, the initial information is shocking and hard to believe; for others, it confirms what they already somehow 'knew'. Most people eventually settle down and accept the diagnosis and comply with the treatment offered, while vacillating between acceptance of the new condition and a reluctance to come to terms with it: 'This can't be happening to me', or 'Why me?' Some people sink into despair; others are stoical, optimistic and hopeful, even to the point of behaving as if the illness did not exist. [...] But is there a right way to cope with information about traumatic, catastrophic or disabling losses?

(Cohen, 2001: 53)

Often the built up expectations of internalised norms regarding mothering, parenting and birth are initially dashed as the parents discover or realise that their child is different from her or his peers. This chapter is about what becoming a mother, or in some cases a father, of an impaired child means for the parents in this research, and what pressures are placed upon them that contribute to feelings of anxiety when faced with emotional and practical difficulty. I often use the term 'parent', but do recognise the (un)gendered significance of this term and yet do not want to dismiss the father's role in mothering. It is clear throughout this chapter that shock, denial and disappointment are experienced in relation to the identification and diagnosis of an impairment. This is an important building block for the following chapters as the reader begins to understand what emotions are experienced *before* any other process of assessment and education is negotiated.

## 'Loss' of the expected child: shock, denial and disappointment

The 24 parents in this research have 30 children between them identified with impairments. Five out of those 30 were diagnosed at birth and one, Kerry, had an ambiguous diagnosis during pregnancy. Tim had difficulty telling people that his son had Down's syndrome; Tracy was not sure how she felt because her son was born visually and hearing impaired and at the time wondered if he should have survived at all, and Kim was simply pleased that her son survived, although she wanted another child soon after so that she could experience the celebration of the birth which she felt she had missed out on. Many of the parents have felt disappointed in the initial stages of their mothering. Even before the birth, though, pressures on mothering and normality are apparent, as illustrated in Kerry's case; the only mother in the sample to have had an official, albeit ambiguous, diagnosis of a potential impairment during pregnancy. The mother and father may fear the death of their child, may be relieved the child is alive, may wish him or her dead (because the impairments cause the baby pain), may deny the impairment and/or experience some kind of shock. The once-expected celebration of the new baby turns into a disappointing loss.

### Discovering difference

After a blood test, during her pregnancy, Kerry was told that she was at high risk of having a baby with Down's syndrome. She arrived at the hospital to have an amniocentesis test, but could not go through with the procedure and told me,

> I thought what am I doing? If this child's normal and they had said that there's a percentage chance that you may abort, you may mis-carriage and lose the baby. And the other thing is it proves the child is Down's so if you don't want the baby you still have to go through with the birth. And I couldn't do that and I didn't want the choice. I didn't want to be given the choice, because the way I looked at it if I hadn't had the injection ... and I was thinking this on the bed ... if I have it and it's not Down's and a few days later I lose it I'd never be able to forgive myself. If I have it and it is Down's I have to decide

whether or not to keep it and I don't think I can do that, I don't think I could do that and say right this child is going to die. I don't think I could do that, so I decided … and I did say to my husband on the way up [to the hospital] if this child is Down's I'm not sure I'll be able to get rid of it and if you want to stay with me you can but you don't have to. He said 'well I can't think like that'.

This clearly demonstrates the conflict of emotions that Kerry was going through related to her feelings about becoming a mother and desiring a normal child, mixed up with the loss of a potentially normal foetus and being unable to put herself in a position to terminate a life if given the 'choice'. Kerry's husband did not want to think at that point about difficulty and termination. He did not want to admit the possibility of an impaired child until he was actually faced with it. She also had little extended family support as her dad had said, 'don't be ridiculous you can't have a Down's child, it'll be too hard you know, it's going to be tied to you for the rest of your life and do you realise all this?' (Kerry). These statements are consistent with common attitudes as can be seen in a survey that asked a 1000 people about their perceptions of those with Down's syndrome, and '[t]he results showed a lack of understanding of the ranges of capability within the syndrome. Life expectancy was consistently considered to be much lower that it actually is' (*Observer Magazine*, 2003). Kerry had prepared herself for what she considered the worst, but in fact when their first son was born he did not have Down's syndrome.

Kerry was relieved because she did not think he 'looked Down's', but she said that the celebration of the birth was tarnished because she was worried about what was going on 'inside his head', based on the abnormal brain waves the health professionals detected during pregnancy. He was diagnosed with epilepsy in the first few months. The paediatrician prescribed a high dose of epilim (a drug for epilepsy), but after two years *Kerry* took him off the drugs and explained,

> my own instinct told me that he was not epileptic … I just knew that, plus we were seeing a cranial osteopath [a complementary therapist] and he advised us and said, 'the chances of him being epileptic were very slim', he just told me what I was thinking anyway.

The emotional angst that many parents, especially the mother, it seems, go through is far greater than the emotional upheaval that is commonly associated with having a new baby ordinarily. Avery (1999: 119), for example, in her study on parenting and disability found the 'case of the mother who fantasized about a 'magic pill' and a pact with the Devil (as trade-offs for her son's inability to walk) suggests a parental obsession with 'normalcy' as the privileged goal for her child'. The shock may seem like obsession, but arguably is common, given the social and cultural pressures placed upon normality. But for some parents, the fact that they may be able to go on to have 'normal' children is enough to get though their current situation.

The bigger shock for Kerry and her husband was not the fact their first son had communication difficulties and was taking drugs for epilepsy, but that their second son began to show similar traits, however without any problems detected during pregnancy, which meant no emotional preparation. Kerry stressed, 'I was absolutely, absolutely devastated, heart broken. Coz I knew ... in fact the funny thing was I probably knew a bit before but I just didn't want to say anything'. This disappointment was specifically about Kerry wanting a 'normal' child and the second son was expected to fill that role. Kim too mentioned wanting another child to fill the normal model, whether that be in the celebration of birth or experiencing a child without impairment. In my own case, I have pondered over what it would be like to mother a child without impairment. Not at the thought of not mothering another child like my daughter, but simply that it would be good (!) to experience the 'normal' – school, homework, tantrums, teenage rebellion and 'independence', and not experience the additional difficulties of countless visits to professionals and sporadic anxiety about her future ad infinitum.

## Shock and denial

Of the other four children identified with an impairment at birth (or very early on in the baby's life), Tim and Karen's babies were diagnosed with Down's syndrome, neither of whom had received this diagnosis during pregnancy. Tim, a father of three who retired early and is the full-time carer of his youngest son, told me that the diagnosis was a huge shock. The way he and his wife were informed was less than sympathetic and the prognosis was particularly negative as seen below. Neither of them knew their baby had Down's syndrome and they were told three days after his birth. Tim spoke of loss, and compared the emotions with that of death when they found out about the diagnosis.

> It's dreadful really ... I think it's like ... possibly when you hear of someone who's died suddenly in a family say, as opposed to an older person. And you really can't believe it ... one part of the shock is that

you really can't believe it ... 'Well perhaps I'll wake up tomorrow and it won't be there', and of course as it goes on and you realise that it will be there and that's part of the shock ... erm, I mean we had a lay idea of what Down's syndrome was like. (The paediatrician) was fairly ... not cold about it, but said something like ... 'well Down's children can *sometimes* do a *small* number of tasks', whereas, yes in reality that's pretty cold.

This clearly suggests that there is an element of both shock and short-term denial. After the initial shock, Tim and his wife wanted to get their baby home as soon as possible to try to have some normality, and in actual fact, because there were no major health issues, found this to be the best option because he was 'just like any other baby' (Tim), especially in the early years.

Karen also wanted to get her baby home as quickly as possible. Karen told me she said to the hospital staff, 'either I take him home within 24 hours or I leave him here and don't take him home at all'. She too had had a bad experience when told about the diagnosis. She was on her own because her husband had already left the hospital for the night. She did have an idea about the diagnosis because of the way her son looked, but thought that all babies with Down's syndrome had a single line in their hand. The paediatrician told her that the line was in his foot instead. Karen explained the only way she got through those two weeks at home while waiting for the test results was to convince herself that her baby did not have Down's syndrome, to deny this possibility, even for a short period of time. By the time the test results had come back, she said, 'he'd been at home so you carry on coping'. Karen had another pregnancy shortly after the birth of her son, but that time had all the tests possible during pregnancy, and was told that the foetus, which was a girl, had a rare disorder and as a result chose to terminate, saying that she did not think she could cope with more than one impaired child.

Denial and shock in relation to the diagnosis and potential loss are common when faced with identification or diagnosis of an impairment not only at birth, but later on in the child's life too, as illustrated by other mothers in this study:

I was totally stunned. Very upset ... it took me back a great deal ... I wanted to hold on to what I knew ... about him, his abilities, you know rather than someone coming in and pulling all that apart ... throwing it all up in the air.

(Babs)

We were just shell-shocked because I had no idea ... that I'd been talking to her for nearly three years and that A, she hadn't been listening and B, she didn't understand.

(Tina)

My husband was just floored and he found it really hard to accept ... him and [my son] have always got on really well and we both knew that he was clever and he said, you know, they should leave him be, and he didn't agree with the interference, he didn't agree with the ... that he was medicated ... but then [my husband] took off really and became less involved.

(Francis)

Denial of the impairment and denial of the actual diagnosis does not always occur, but if it does can take on very different forms. Many of the parents in this research, including myself, have been through some kind of denial. According to Cohen (2001: 6), '[t]he mind somehow grasps what is going on – but rushes a protective filter into place'. Seligman and Darling (1997: 93), with regard to parents with disabled children suggest, '[d]enial serves as a useful, buffering purpose early on but can cause difficulties if it persists'. For Karen it was immediate, and she really did not want to admit that her son had Down's syndrome because she was scared that she would not want to take him home. It was safer for her to get out of the hospital, deny what was feared and spend the time mothering her son, and indeed bonding.

Denial shows itself in different ways but the most common manifestation of it in this research is what Cohen (2001) would call 'interpretive denial'. Where something has happened, for instance, identification and diagnosis has taken place, but as yet the parent is unable to confront the full meaning and places the difficulty into a less severe bracket. A child identified with ASD may still be thought of as having *only* a speech and language difficulty, not a *learning* impairment. Cohen (2001: 7–8) talks about denial in relation to lessening the problem, for example, in the case of an alcoholic they may claim to be, only a social drinker. 'It disputes the cognitive meaning given to an event and re-allocates it to another class of event'. Denial of a learning disability, intellectual impairment or low intelligence quotient (IQ) has been common among the mothers and fathers in this research based on their cultural assumptions of 'handicap'. It seems that having low intelligence is the worst impairment possible for many parents. In my own case, for years, I denied that my daughter's difficulties were anything *more* than dyslexia. Not that I am trying to minimalise dyslexia, as in itself it can be a difficult impairment. I guess at the time, on a scale of impairment, I was searching and hoping for an impairment that I thought would have the least impact on the rest of my daughter's life negatively. I did not want to associate my daughter with others commonly labelled 'mentally retarded', despite the fact that she clearly had other learning impairments too.

While many of the parents accept their child may have learning *difficulties*, they deny that they are 'that bad' or are indeed intellectually impaired (see also Chapter 5). Even though Lynne, a mother of two boys one of whom has AS and epilepsy, did not discover her son had impairments until later on, she emphasised the importance and privileging of intellectual ability. She said she was mortified when told her son had a low IQ.

> I don't know how to put it really. I think the worst point was I think he was about 11 and he saw the ed psych at the primary school and I think we were coming up to the sensory test and then she actually put a figure on his IQ and that was I think ... she said it was 70, 75 and I couldn't believe it. I think that was the worst point really because I'd been reading quite a bit and I know that you could have Down's syndrome and have an IQ of 70 and I just looked at her and said, 'but kids with Down's syndrome ... can have an IQ of 70'. I just looked at her shocked. And she said, 'Down's syndrome can have an IQ higher than that you know'. I wished I hadn't asked sometimes. I think she thought she was telling me good news, she said, 'your son will be able to live an independent life and he will be able to look after himself' [she raises her voice]. *I hadn't thought that he wouldn't! You know!* Sometimes I think they [the professionals] are further ahead in the game than you are [laughs]. You know I was shell shocked, absolutely shell shocked. I think then I went home I got under the duvet and cried myself stupid. I thought, 'I've got a disabled child'. And I know he's 11 but nobody had ever said anything like that to me before.

This reaction implies there are levels of *acceptable difficulties* and those that are not, in other words, hierarchies of impairment.

Kerry initially denied that her children had any learning impairments, both of whom now attend a residential school for verbal dyspraxia and other related problems. She did not consider her children to be 'disabled' in any way at the time of the first interview and said that she would be the first to admit she did not want to face it, and denied the fact that her two boys were different from the average. Her reaction to this difference when she visited a special school was quite graphic.

> When I first walked into the school I straight away thought, 'oh my god these are physically and mentally handicapped'. Excuse the expression but they were dribbling, their eyes were rolling, they were they were to my opinion an extreme, extreme case of problems, erm ... some of them were making noises, some of them were running all over the place and I found it quite frightening, what would Ian feel like. Because it's ... it's not normal, it's not normal to any of us if I were really honest and you know I do feel strongly that if every parent was honest with themselves and with other people they would not want their child that only has speech problems mixing with children like that. And I know that does sound awful and I know that but I'm being honest. I'm being honest with myself, and being honest with people around me.

Kerry went through a lot of changes in how she considered both of her sons' impairments but this is how she described her initial reactions, a defence in the early stages of coming to terms with, or denying the severity of impairments that a child may have. A need to hang on to some 'normality' is often graded in relation to more severe impairments, and then disassociated from that category.

## Disappointment

Not all parents deny their child's impairments, and in some cases it is impossible to do so, in these instances parents may question their ability to cope. Tracy did not experience denial, having been given what seemed like a clear diagnosis at the birth of her first son (a twin, the other one was born without impairments). When her son was born, she was told that her older twin had hydrocephalus (or water in the brain), as well as other impairments. She said, 'he was totally blind, totally deaf ... erm ... and like changing his nappy was like, although he was warm it was like a dead body, erm ... he couldn't even blink we had to put drops in his eyes. He was still on the ventilator at this point' and continued,

> I got to the stage before we were told he got meningitis, we went through everything else ... I sometimes looked at him *willing him to give up*. Because ... the temperature thing they have on him, if they leave that on for more than four hours that leaves a burn. And with the hustle and bustle of the unit, if there was an emergency, these

monitors didn't get moved on to a different part of the body so he did get burnt, and I'm thinking he's getting burnt and it was like cigarette burns so he must have been in pain.

Clearly, Tracy was not sure if she wanted her baby to survive based on her assumptions about his pain and trauma, but this experience was also traumatic and emotionally painful for her. She did feel guilty for wanting her son to die but rationalised it based on not wanting him to suffer. However, she did not give up on him and now feels good about that. At the time of the first interview her son was a healthy young man at mainstream college (although still wears a shunt in his skull), no longer visually or hearing impaired, and is physically independent.

Regarding disappointment then, the emotional pain of coming to terms with the 'loss' of the child the parents thought they were going to have, the lack of celebration, and the future that in many ways parents subconsciously map out, has been destroyed and a different future has to be negotiated as in the case of all the parents in this research. Some parents take longer in negotiating that future than others. Kim had feelings of loss, especially with regard to the celebration of the eagerly anticipated first child. Her oldest son was identified with impairments at birth and had a very vulnerable start to his life. Initially she was told that her son might die as he was born at 26 weeks, had numerous brain bleeds and was told he could be visually impaired too. However, the actual diagnosis of cerebral palsy was not discussed and Kim explained,

> I stumbled across it. I think it was put on his medical card and I didn't realise that's what he'd [the paediatrician] said. I'm sure no one actually said he'd got it, and the physio said, 'there's differences there' I think I read his medical card and I read some notes on him and I thought, 'oh is that what it is then?'

Kim was disappointed in having what she considered an 'abnormal baby'. 'I was really disappointed that my first baby wasn't … you know … perfect. But once I'd got over that', she said she was fine, and wanted another child.

> Because I wanted it to be right this time and I suppose what it was is you have this fairy tale in your mind where you get married and you have a baby and you push a pram around and you are going to have this beautiful baby that is gorgeous and lovely and cooing and all that, and its just an illusion and it's just something that little girls

have and then that illusion was shattered but I did cope all right with it. I noticed it was a big bubble that went … 'oh forget that Kim, it's not going to be like that again', and I suppose I must have wanted that and when [her next son] came along I was overwhelmed with the fact that he was well and healthy and I could take him out of the hospital within three days, and I kept looking at him in wonder.

Tina too, in relation to disappointment, recalled how she reacted when her daughter was diagnosed with a language disorder.

We took the children to Burger King that night and both of us were in tears, because although we, we barely knew what it was [language disorder] we both realised that this was … she wasn't going to grow up, get married and have children and get a job in the way we always imagined. We did realise the implications of it straight away.

Disappointment may be associated with dashed expectations, a common theme that cuts across this research. Something occurs in one's life that was unexpected. Craib (1994: 44) suggests,

Disappointment comes not only from having to restrict ourselves from having to share with other people and from having to make choices in our lives; it also comes from the recognition of what we are, and it is not a world shattering announcement that we are not always what we might like to think we are.

Significantly, this links into what Beck and Beck-Gernsheim (2001: 105) suggest. Having children is 'increasingly connected with hopes of being rooted, of life becoming meaningful, and with a "claim to happiness", based on the close relationship with the child'. What can be argued here is that these parents who have children identified and diagnosed with impairments are often stripped of their hopes and dreams as well as questioning their own abilities. Parents may recognise this disappointment in themselves as parents who have produced a 'less than perfect' child, as Kim states here when thinking about the birth. 'I didn't ever celebrate his birth'.

Impairments such as medical or health problems, Down's syndrome and, sometimes, cerebral palsy (depending on severity) may be more easily identifiable at birth and therefore the child and the family become involved with professionals from the start. They begin a process of coming to terms with the impairment and in some cases renegotiate life paths, as in the case of Tracy, with countless visits to the hospital and medical procedures she had to learn. And Kim became her son's physiotherapist. (See Chapter 6 in discussing 'professional parenting'). Identification of an impairment at birth suggests that the health professionals have diagnosed the impairment but many parents feel that there are problems or difficulties *before* any professional does. In the following section I unpack this and engage with those parents who have themselves discovered or identified a difference.

## Parental identification, emotional responses and labels

Half of the parents in this study had a feeling that something was 'not quite right' with their baby or young child before a health or education professional had identified an impairment. Some mothers, including Kerry for example, claimed that they definitely had a 'maternal instinct' with regard to their children, as Kerry commented 'how else would I know more about my children than the so called expert'. This section is about the parents' stories of identifying an impairment (or difficulty) and procuring a label.

### Parental identification

As said, half the participants in this study said they knew something was 'not quite right' with their baby and yet had difficulties convincing the health professionals. Tracy for example, with her fourth child (but the second with impairments), told me,

> Brad was fine for a couple of months and then I felt something wasn't quite right. He couldn't hold his head up ... wouldn't give eye contact at all and really strange smiles ... everyone found it amusing but I found it quite sinister, even at six weeks he would start laughing ... so I was backwards and forwards with health visitors and the others saying he'll catch up ... this was going on from a few months old, right through to when I finally got someone to say, yes there was something wrong with him ... it wasn't what was wrong with him, but that was at three and a half.

It was not until Brad was 10 years old that he was diagnosed with a rare syndrome, the symptoms of which meant that he would be infertile and have some kind of EBD. As a result of setting fire to his primary school and a culmination of previous disruptive events he was placed in a residential school.

Lynne too indicated that she knew something was not quite right and echoed Tracy.

> I knew right from the start but ... he, he, he was different to other babies .... I've always thought that was one of the hardest things ... trying to prove to other people that there's something wrong with your child, when they insist on telling you there's something wrong with you! [laughs].

Lynne was told her son was a 'late developer', and initially felt she was to blame. She was told by an education professional that her son would be able to live independently which was the first time they had indicated there were problems and this shocked her. At the age of 10 he was diagnosed with epilepsy and at 14 he was diagnosed with childhood autism, but later was told it was AS. Both of these examples illustrate that even if the mother has a feeling that something might not be quite right, trying to convince others was not always simple.

As illustrated above, Kerry told me she thought she had an 'instinctual' knowledge about her children, and others have said, 'he was fine for a couple of months and then I felt something wasn't quite right' (Tracy). 'Well I had an idea, but I let it be because they were such small things' (Francis). 'I say, I knew right from the start ... he was different to other babies' (Lynne). 'He didn't really seem to have sort of muscles that ... didn't seem to support him ...' (Stella). All of these children were identified as having one or more of the following: ASD, dyspraxia, dyslexia, SPLD, AD/HD, AS and a rare syndrome. Importantly, the majority of these conditions are difficult, if not impossible, to diagnose at birth. Apart from the 'rare syndrome' none are identifiable by a blood test, and are often only identifiable when learning, speech, language and social and/ or behavioural difficulties emerge. Furthermore, '[m]edical knowledge simply is not yet at the point where all childhood disabilities can be definitively labelled' (Seligman and Darling, 1997: 47). With regard to labelling, all parents in this research wanted a label for their child's impairment, although not all wanted the particular label initially given to them by education or health professionals.

### Identification and diagnosis

Parents in this study who suspected their child had some kind of impairment still went through the shock, denial and disappointment that other parents with a clear diagnosis at birth went through, but their difficulties were often exacerbated by feelings of paranoia because health professionals did not initially take these parental feelings about a difference on board, or simply because parents had assumed their child was not different. Even if the parents had a feeling that something was not quite right, in some cases, they often did not expect the diagnosis that came with the eventual identification of the impairment.

Neil, whose third child was diagnosed with ASD, believed that his son 'progressed normally' up until he had the Measles, Mumps and Rubella (MMR) immunisation. Neil explained that since the MMR immunisation his son had lost what little understanding of language he had, and that he simply did not respond if asked to do something. It would be fair to say that Neil's reaction to the 'official' identification of his son's impairment was not unusual, but he described the experience vividly here.

> You think 'oh god it's gonna be something else' and you just thought 'oh please let it be that' and it wasn't ... we went across the doctors again and you get 'oh he's a boy' and 'he'll be delayed' and 'he'll be alright' and that's why it's still quite a shock that when you actually do, I think he was about two and a half you go from 'oh it's all alright' and you take him to the child development centre and they say 'well this is either severe language impairment or it's mild autism, what do you think about that'? And you think ... eh? You know; hang on a minute you've just punched me in the face with something.

Both he and his wife began to question their parenting skills at that point. They were shocked and disappointed at being told their son would have significant difficulties.

As we have heard above, this shock and disappointment is also about being stripped of the future they had assumed, added to which they felt unsupported in their diagnosis. Neil disclosed to me that there were no real support structures in place when parents receive a diagnosis of this sort.

> This is one of the things my wife, she said, 'if you're told you have breast cancer or if you're told you have any other sort of cancers you're offered counselling' but it wasn't ... it's just you know you're told this, and 'have you got any questions'? *'Have I got any questions'?!* I mean 'what do you mean I can't think straight you know you've just told me' ... all I could feel was like to me it's like that moment in Jaws when that bloke's sat on the beach and suddenly the camera zooms in on him and you know you're him and like I don't know how to react to this you know you're telling me my son's ...

what autistic? You're telling me my child's just ... not have things that other children have, you've, you've stripped ... you don't realise in your subconscious you've got these things and like at least a child when they're older they can make their own decisions, they'll decide their job, they can decide if they get married, or not, they can decide if they have a car, or not, 'you've suddenly said to me that's it'. That's what it felt like.

For Neil, there was a grieving process, as well as shock, which manifested itself in not wanting to engage with the difficulties. Cohen (2001: 10) would call this 'personal denial' where the denial appears to be wholly individual. For example, 'spouses who put aside suspicions about their partner's infidelities', or refuse to believe that a family member could commit child abuse are types of personal denial. For many of the parents in my research this 'personal denial' may only last a short while. Some of the mothers have expressed this, too, when talking about the father's reaction to their child's identification of impairment. Those couples who have remained together seem to have different ways of dealing with the diagnosis in the early days, and some of the mothers inter-viewed claimed that it took the father a little longer to come to terms with the diagnosis of an impairment.

As we have already heard in the previous section Francis said that her husband initially withdrew from the parental role quite significantly. Neil responded by going out with his friends.

I didn't want to talk about it [his son's impairment] I just I went into a shell for at least, probably about a month I couldn't talk, I didn't want to talk, well I wanted to talk bollocks, let's talk football, get pissed I don't want to talk about it [his son's diagnosis] anymore.

Tina, another mother who thought there was something wrong, reiter-ates this initial reaction and explained,

you go through the shock, the denial, the grief for the child that you thought you had ... gradually you come to terms with the difficulties realising that you've got to get up and fight for the provisions they need and this takes about two years and at the end of that two years they've [the father] probably taken it on board although the pain never goes away altogether and the fathers are possibly just begin-ning to acknowledge there's a problem.

Neil too revealed this in relation to a grieving process.

> You grieve for the child that you wish you had, you no longer ... you
> don't ... you certainly ... you think well this is my son, you know as
> a dad like but I want to take him to football, but I want to do this,
> you know, I want to do that, and now I think of course I can still do
> those ... you stupid bastard...! You know, you know but at the time
> you just feel sorry for yourself and you think, why did I feel sorry for
> myself? It's him who's having a problem, not me!

Neil describes his loss and the emotional conflicts very clearly here. The
emotional struggles that the parents go through during this period of
identification and diagnosis often feel insurmountable, and yet it seems
that these emotions are part of a process of accepting that their baby
may not be the one they had imagined or expected.

### To label or not to label?

For some of the parents who identified a problem, there seemed to be a
time of loss, grief and denial that manifested in different ways and at
different times, but in the main, while the pain may reoccur at different
transitional stages, acceptance settled. This could take weeks, months or
years. However, others may feel some grief at the diagnosis, and also
feel relieved about the diagnosis because their thoughts about the 'differences' had finally been recognised. This is mainly because until an
impairment is recognised by health or education professionals the
mother or father often blame themselves for unusual behaviour or slow
development. They are in fact looking for a label to confirm their suspicions and find a point of reference so they are able to look forward.
Stella suggested that a label 'helps you to help support their needs.
When it's inconsistent (the label) it's hard to know what support to give
at that time'. Without such a label parents often feel unable to fully support their child.

Seligman and Darling (1997: 47) suggest that in such cases where the
parents have suspected a problem they are relieved at the diagnosis and
illustrate,

> When the doctor told us he couldn't believe how well we accepted the
> diagnosis. All I can say is that it was such a relief to have someone
> finally just come out and say what we had feared for so long! We felt
> now that we could move ahead and do the best we could for Timmy.

And again,

> When James turned six months old, my husband and I decided to
> change paediatricians. The second doctor was an angel in disguise.
> She spotted the problem immediately. ... The reason I call her an
> angel was that she finally put an end to the unknown. The not know-
> ing exactly what was wrong was driving me crazy.
>
> > (ibid.)

For Tina, in this research, although the diagnosis was devastating,

> in a way it was a relief that a professional has put into words, we had
> no idea about language disorders, dyspraxia and this is someone who
> said this is what it is.

The label can often be useful in the whole process of coming to terms
with the identification of an impairment and then being able to talk
about it. Babs exclaimed that finally gaining a label was not only liberat-
ing but a point of reference to talk to her husband about the difficulties.

> It was wonderful because ... this is not strange, this is not a child
> who doesn't fit in the box, this is how he is. So then it was much eas-
> ier to talk to my husband about this and say well actually there is a
> name for it.

Sociologically, there has been a long tradition on labelling, especially
in relation to deviance, and it is often assumed to be a negative process
associated with stigma (Barnes et al., 1999; Becker, 1963 [1973]; Goffman,
1969; Gray, 2002). I am not denying there are negative connotations in
relation to labels, with stigma, however many of the participants in this
research have spent a great deal of time and money pursuing a label for
the impairment their child has. Whether for peace of mind or for gaining
the most appropriate support, it was often the 'experts' report that made
the difference. Tina spoke to me about her overdraft with the bank and
how much money she and her husband had spent. 'The educational
psychologist and her report were £1300 and the speech therapist ...'
Lynne explained after realising that she needed a specific label to procure funding and support.

> [The psychologist] just chatted to Kevin for about half an hour and
> said Asperger's syndrome and wrote me a lovely report. A three page
> report which was absolutely brilliant, and I was so impressed with

him ... I suppose if you've got the money and you get the right person you are paying for that person to write the thing that you want them to write. But that's life.

The label at the time of identification and diagnosis is often not considered by the parents as a life long tag that the child will then need to negotiate as an adult, but that of a tool to aid understanding and procure appropriate support and/or therapy. As in my case, I recall paying for a private assessment and therapy for my daughter, by which time it was the middle of 1995. She was nine years old; we were still visiting the (centre) every six weeks, which was between £60 and £100 a visit. This involved not only money but also time, to and from London. It also clearly indicates that if parents are financially stable they are more likely to be able to 'buy' a label or at least the assessment.

Within her cultural and social sphere the specific diagnosis aids the mother's, and often the father's, own parental 'research' and acceptance of what problems their child may have in the hope that there are specific resources and ways to support and help them and their child in the assessment and education process. It also gives the parents an entry point at which to begin to understand, and therefore accept the difficulties. Within a political sphere the label seems an all-important tool in aiding the most appropriate provision for the child's educational and emotional support via the LEA. Without this, the child, parents, school and teachers are left without appropriate funding and support for each child's needs.

Within the English and Welsh education context labels have been discussed in the SENCO-FORUM (2003a: 107) and although there are some who totally reject labels, many, particularly those who have children with impairments, have found them essential. 'They had found that giving a label to a child's need was an essential passport to obtaining resources for help'. Not only is the label a ticket to resources but there is also 'a perception that labels have a significant effect on the way individuals are regarded by others, and also how they regard themselves' (ibid.). This feeds into the public perception of difference, difficulty and impairment, but also as stated here, on the emotional experience of being associated with disability and impairment.

Labels mean different things to different people and how medical professionals use labels can also make a huge difference to how parents react to the labels used. There is a common theme that the parents in this research reiterate: a diagnosis with a label attached can help the parents to research the difficulty and gain some control over the situation. Debbie, who felt her son had problems, told me that 'no one would put a label on him, nobody will put you in a particular box and no body gave him any help'. Many of the parents while questioning labels realise that if they do not have a label then support is not forthcoming as suggested here; 'unless a child is labelled they don't get any help' (Marlene).

There can sometimes be a more instrumental attitude towards the label itself as illustrated by Lynne above, when explaining about 'paying for the label', and Mary said that the label originally given to her son was that of AD/HD, but she was actually trying to get a diagnosis of ASD because she was aware of the negative assumptions about 'bad parenting' around AD/HD and explained,

> I mean they're always negative ... AD/HD everybody thinks they're little bastards, s'cuse me for that, but they do. 'Oh no they're hyper active' and the teacher thinks 'oh no' and all they get is the paper-work with that written all over it, 'oh god here's another useless parent who gives their kid sugar for breakfast and then blames the world'. Ok so that's what they think! I know it! I know lots of teachers; I know that's what they think! But if they see autistic there's more knowledge in educational psychology and.... There's more empathy ... there certainly is a better understanding of autism and acceptance that it's a real condition whereas AD/HD they don't really accept it as real.

Mary was not too interested in a label per se, but knew the label would aid her in procuring the most appropriate support for her son in school. She wanted to be taken seriously and had her own negative perceptions about AD/HD, which were fuelled by professional responses to the label. She wanted a label that professionals would take seriously regardless of her son's actual difficulties. However, even though Mary felt there was something wrong, before she could come to terms with the fact that her son may actually have ASD, she also went through denial of this and said,

> I guess I refused to see him as autistic even though the signs were there, but I think that it was my knowledge of autism was not sufficient so people would say. ... My mum said it ... she was the first person to say it to me actually. She said he's kinda like someone who's deaf because he was very monosyllabic and no emotion in his speech ... I said, 'look he likes to be cuddled, he likes to play, he likes to do stuff, he's got social ability ... he's not autistic ...' it was about eight or nine months later I said to the paediatrician 'cards on the table time'.

The paediatrician did tell her that he had some autistic tendencies at that point, but was reticent to diagnose.

Unlike the parents above, the parents who had the diagnosis of an impairment *at birth* did not have to prove any differences to gain a label. However the label, and in fact the diagnosis of an impairment at birth, does not necessarily mean the child or the family automatically gains additional support. The following section explores parents' narratives in documenting the effects on them as the professional, not the mother, initiates the identification and diagnosis of the impairment.

## Professional diagnosis

As discussed, I have documented those parents who thought there were problems with their child from very early on, or in fact had an identification of impairment at birth, and parents who initiated an identification. Parents however do not always know about the impairment and throughout the early months and years can assume their child is no different from any other. This can especially be the case with such impairments as dyslexia, attention difficulties and AS, for example. Over a third of the participants' children in this study did not have a diagnosis of impairment until they had started primary school or later. Five parents told me they did not think there were any problems and were shocked when the health or education professionals told them there were. Significantly, except for Babs, all had not had children before, indicating these parents had no previous experiences to measure development by.

Una illustrates the emotional content with regard to the late diagnosis in relation to grief and argues that these emotions leave the mother feeling very angry and often with nowhere to vent it, except on those professionals or on other family members. For her, every developmental test showed that her son was just within 'normal' range, nothing was identified and she did not get a final diagnosis until he was eight years old. By which time she claimed that she did not want to know because the diagnosis then seemed too severe. Una explained that sometimes by the time the difficulty is identified and diagnosed the parents often believe that maybe the problems are not that bad or they would have been identified and diagnosed earlier. She explained, when one does finally receive a diagnosis, a period of grief is needed.

> Grieving is a form of anger. There's no getting away from it, when you're told your child has a form of disability no matter what the disability is, what level it's at you will go through some form of grieving,

you can't escape that. And grief normally takes the form of anger and there are a lot of angry parents out there, and the professionals have to deal with them and that's very difficult for them.

Disappointment denial, disappointment, loss and grief in the early stages of a diagnosis are then compounded with feelings of anxiety about the impairment.

### Shock and late diagnosis

Babs actually thought she had a genius on her hands not an impaired child, and revealed,

> without a word of exaggeration there were times when we thought we'd got a genius. We actually thought we'd got a very clever child, because he was very advanced in virtually everything. ... Which made it doubly difficult to find out we hadn't. ...

She later said she had felt humiliated for thinking she had a bright child. 'It's like I'd been taken in. It's like being deceived ... it's a very cruel condition'. Her son was diagnosed with AS at the age of 10 and epilepsy at the age of 13 and a half. Initially a teacher had called her in to tell of the concerns that her son was misbehaving. This was a complete shock, as she considered herself and family to be conformist. But she recalled a really bad day when she had a visit from the health visitor.

> I just remember a devastating day when she was here, he was playing about and she said, 'have you considered the fact that he might be autistic?' and I think by then I had begun to reach my own conclusions, at the same time knowing there's a grain of truth but also ... but how can he be because everyone's idea of what autism was ... was not what he was. I wanted to hold on to what I knew ... about him, his abilities, you know rather than somebody coming in and pulling all that apart and throwing it up in the air.

Babs told me her husband became particularly defensive about the diagnosis and wanted *proof* of an impairment.

Not only do these parents have to deal with the very late diagnosis, they also need to deal with what happens next or indeed what one does with the feelings of loss and initial shock.

> People learn to cope with it but you feel it's not real ... and loss, I suppose all that joy ... achievements ... going to college ... that's all

suddenly been snatched away. I suppose I transferred that on to the wicked people who were trying to help him [laughs].

(Babs)

Often in these cases, the professionals are used as scapegoats by the parents and a lot of anger is directed towards them, however it is a relationship that requires understanding and empathy not conflict. The emotional intensity and often the lack of funding that surrounds government provision can cause explosive meetings between parents and professionals. What often lies at the root of the difficulty in this parent–professional relationship is the intensity of emotion experienced. (The parent–professional 'partnership' is discussed further in the following chapter). This emotional intensity is not only experienced at the time of a diagnosis but throughout the child's life as suggested here in Gascoigne's (1995: 12) research.

> One would have expected that, after eleven years of covering his [her son's] history with various professionals, time and frequency of retelling would have inured me to the full emotional reaction. Part way through recounting the history, I was bewildered as to why this professional, and my husband, were looking at me with increasing concern on their faces, and could not understand why the words in my head were failing to come out through my mouth. Eventually, my husband leaned over, took my hand and said, 'Stop trying to talk'. Only then did I realise that I was crying, the tears rolling down my cheeks, my eyes getting redder and redder, my voice cracking. It took me almost twenty minutes to recover sufficiently to rejoin the conversation, which my husband had been able to pick up in the mean time.

This example not only illustrates an intensity of emotion, but also the importance of another person (maybe the father, a partner, friend or relative) in support at these meetings. A parent may think they have dealt with certain aspects of their child's difficulties but a meeting, a new diagnosis or simply transitional stages can tap into all of those early emotions around loss and disappointment.

As with Babs, some children receive identification and/or diagnosis of impairment when they are already at school because their behaviour seems different to the other children, or their academic performance is not progressing at a certain developmental rate. In my case, because I did not think my daughter had a significant learning impairment I was particularly hard on her in those early school years. She would come home with spellings to learn and I would get frustrated and angry because she would not remember any of them. I would constantly shout at her for losing track, not concentrating, leaving things at school, not grasping the simplest of concepts, being too slow to dress in the mornings, eating messily and so on. She did not particularly want to go to school, unsurprisingly, as everything seemed a blur of sounds and vision. Even though I had an identification of an impairment at birth, it cannot be assumed the parent has accepted that the child will *not* develop intellectually.

## The dyslexic continuum

Kathy had four children; her two oldest sons were identified with severe dyslexia. She did not notice there were any problems with her oldest until he was 13 years old when he was diagnosed with severe dyslexia. While her children's impairments may seem less profound than some of the other participants' children, she told me she 'felt cheated that nothing was done before' and equally while there are other children who have multiple impairments she was only interested in her children, and simply wanted them to gain the best possible education. Her sons had to face ridicule for taking extra lessons at school, which was the cause of much heartache at home. She explained, 'he [her oldest] gets bullied and found it very hard to cope with ...' but went on and told me, 'it's nice to know what is wrong'.

Identification of an impairment can affect parents in many different ways and the severity of the impairment does not directly correlate with how a parent deals with the impact of a diagnosis. I met Kathy as part of my participant observation in a joint 'LEA/support charity' parents meeting, and she was in my group and agreed to be interviewed. She was very upset that evening and I noticed she was crying (but tried to hide the fact). She did not feel part of the group because her sons' impairments seemed less significant than the others in the group. In our group of parents, a father proclaimed, 'so we can assume that all our children have statements here then?' (Personal research journal, 2002). Because Kathy's children did not have statements, even though they had been identified with SEN, she had mixed emotions between feeling fraudulent for attending the meeting based on the horror stories some parents told, and wanting to be there because she too had problems in dealing with her emotional responses and difficulties that her sons' impairments caused her and them.

Like Kathy, both of Trisha's children were on the dyslexic continuum and she had not been told that her oldest son was receiving support in the classroom. She was completely shocked at the identification of the impairment, which took place at a parents' evening.

It was fortunate that my husband came as well because we both came out of the meeting going 'oh my word what on earth's the matter'. You know shocked, we were thinking why isn't he like everyone else, why can't he do these things because they're all saying, the teacher, the special needs teacher says he socialises fine, he's got lots of friends erm … you know well behaved, no behavioural problem. [Very quiet]. Such a shame because if he'd been noisy and misbehaved [she said sarcastically] *SO* much more would have been done earlier [laughs] but it was then when we went home and thought 'what's a specific learning difficulty?'

Often before the diagnosis and label, the parents can feel out of control. Katy's husband, who was with her in the interview said, 'we didn't know what the problem was. At least if you know the starting point of what the problem was, what you're dealing with …'

Again labelling has been indicated as an important aspect in the diagnosis of an impairment as emphasised by Babs.

Well I have a problem with this label thing. I only seem to hear it from someone who doesn't want to give you a diagnosis. It's just used as an excuse … Not to give a diagnosis. 'I don't like the word label' [her doctor said], 'Why not … this condition'…? You don't not say someone's not got cancer, if you label them you've either got it or you haven't! It's like you can't be a little bit pregnant. You are or you're not. It strikes me that term is only ever used by a power that doesn't want to assign someone the appropriate level of provision or level of service. Because it would mean implications for them. It's all very well the psychologist saying this … but if you don't label him he wont get the help … if you don't diagnose him, or identify him … or whatever other word you want to use. It's been picked up as a convenient cop out.

However, both parents and professionals need to be able to negotiate together, and coming to terms with an impairment is not a straightforward process on which one can place a time limit. I paid for an assessment when my daughter was eight years old because the education professionals did not want to assess her. Eventually she was given a diagnosis of dyspraxia and moderate learning disability. At the time I had no idea what that meant, but went out and bought literature on dyspraxia. Recognising idiosyncratic behaviour articulated by others is often part of the process in coming to terms with an identification, whether early on or after the child has begun the education process.

## Conclusions

This chapter has explored the experiences of mothers and fathers during the identification and diagnosis of their child's impairment. It suggests that internalised norms and the social pressures on parents and especially mothers to produce 'perfect' babies and meet all their needs are immense. As Ribbens (1994: 54–5) in her research on childrearing illustrates:

> Mary suggested that a mother should seek to love her children as 'they are', even if they had characteristics that mother found hard to accept – It's very important to love them for what they are. You see people trying to change people and you shouldn't. Such acceptance is more difficult, of course, if a new baby does not live up to a woman's expectations, whether in terms of gender, physical attractiveness, or dis/ability.

This acceptance does not always happen immediately, as in the case of some of the parents in this research. I have found that when a mother or father is faced with the identification of an impairment she or he may feel shock, loss, grief and disappointment to name but a few of the emotions. The emotional experience of actually being told, discovering or the parent feeling that something is 'not quite right' with their baby or child can cause emotional anxiety and conflict for both the parents and the professionals. All of these emotions are part of the diagnosis and identification process, and it is not one that can be described as chronological. These emotions can reoccur at any time, and begs the question, does it make a difference on the emotional impact when the diagnosis or identification takes place? Significantly, those children who were identified or diagnosed with an impairment at birth or early on were more likely to have a visible impairment such as Down's syndrome and/or cerebral palsy.

This emotional roller coaster that parents experience is predominantly about perceived expectations that include giving birth to a 'normal' child, the expected celebrations and imagined future of their child. Furthermore, the internalised norms of the mothering process and all that comes with it places an even greater pressure on parents who have children with impairments. What I am not suggesting here, though, is that the emotional impact on discovery of an impairment is one of a linear process whereby the above feelings happen and trigger the next one in some kind of a cycle. But that these feelings can happen sporadically and occur in a messy and unpredictable way, which are sometimes repeated time and again, as in the case cited in Gascoigne (1995) and reiterated in other research on families with an impaired child (Avery, 1999; Emerson, 2003; Maes et al., 2003 and Read, 2000). I am reminded of this as my daughter moves past her nineteenth birthday and again I ponder over her future. I sometimes feel sad at the future she will not have, but also feel blessed to have such a great daughter. I also look forward to her future, as she continues her further education.

This chapter highlights that those parents who have already had a child are more likely to have an inkling that their baby or child may have difficulties. Children with impairments such as AS, dyslexia, dyspraxia and related impairments are unlikely to be diagnosed with an impairment at birth. However, whether the diagnosis is at birth or later on, mothers and fathers in the main still go through many, if not all, of the above emotions and often at some point come into conflict with professionals. Contrary to sociological literature on labelling and the pejorative effects (Barnes, 1999; Becker, 1963/1973; Goffman, 1963), all parents in this research have wanted a label that will aid their understanding of their child's impairment, enable them to talk to others about the impairment (including their partners), and also procure support from external agencies. Furthermore, the label gives meaning to difficulties incurred that surround the impairment. This chapter outlined all the above affects and introduced the reader to some of the participants involved in this study. The following chapter moves beyond the initial diagnosis (although none of this process is chronological and linear and so therefore may cover initial diagnosis for those who discovered the impairment later on) and engages with the parents' stories as they move on to the 'official' assessment process.

# 4

# Statementing and Partnership: Working Together?

> The involvement of parents in the assessment processes
> for special education, and the actual education of their
> children in special schools and classes, is an area in
> which benevolent rhetoric supersedes reality. While
> government publications and professional groups urge
> the involvement of parents as equals, the available evi-
> dence indicates that many parents feel uninvolved and
> inadequately consulted in the assessment processes and
> uninformed, misinformed or overwhelmed by profes-
> sional expertise when their children are actually placed
> in special education.
>
> (Tomlinson, 1982: 106)

This quote from Sally Tomlinson written over two decades ago is still relevant in the 21st century. This chapter unfolds how this is the case, via
stories from the parents who took part in this research. It moves the parents from identification and diagnosis, as the previous chapter described,
to how parents deal with the official processes they become involved in
(whether that involves to educate, support or manage a difficulty).

This chapter is divided into four sections, and the first section begins
by describing some common experiences of the assessment and statementing process. The second section is about how the *family* are identified as the problem rather than the child, and how this is one route to
an assessment and possible statement. The third documents the
extreme legal battles that can be incurred if a statement is refuted by the
parents. And in the final section I discuss the culmination of the actual
conflict described. The conflict is in the parents' expectation of partnership based on pamphlets and policy, for example, in the Green Paper

(DfEE, 1997a), 'Excellence for All Children' where partnership with parents is positioned as important, if not vital.

## The assessment and statementing process

The statement of SEN (or 'record of needs' in Scotland) is a legally binding document that every child who has been assessed and identified with educational needs above and beyond those of his or her peers is currently entitled to in England and Wales. A statement of SEN involves a statutory assessment process whereby the LEA, parents, teachers or health professionals collate certain information about a child and his or her difficulties and needs. This triggers the involvement of other professionals (if not already involved) such as educational psychologists (EPs), special educational needs coordinators (SENCOs), social workers, speech therapists, occupational therapists and medical professionals. The significance of this statement, or at least the assessment of specific social and educational needs, is such that without it the child may be left unsupported without the appropriate structures in place to maintain the most appropriate education package. It is therefore the child's and parents' right to expect that once a child has been identified with difficulties in learning, for example, the assessment process is triggered. Understandably, not all parents realise this, or are aware of the legally binding implications of such a document.

The following box(box [4.1]) is a guide to the route in the assessment and statementing identified as a bigger *family* problem. However, if after this route the 'experts' dismiss the family as the causal problem, the route to the statement will either begin at the top of the left hand column or where the statutory assessment begins further down the left hand column.

Five children in my sample, although identified with SEN, did not have statements, two were in the process of assessment, and one mother had not accepted the statement (at the time of interview) and was appealing the decision, but her children were on the LEA's 'stages of need'. (Now called 'School Action' and School Action Plus). The Audit Commission (2002: 6–7) highlights the fact that in England there were no common definitions of need. So while LEAs held detailed records of the children in their geographical area, the data could not be aggregated, and yet in Wales and Scotland there are detailed statistics of children who have statements (or 'records of needs' in Scotland) with their 'type of need'. For example, out of the children in Wales with statements, five per cent have been identified with ASD, eight per cent have

## Box 4.1 The process of assessment and statementing for SEN

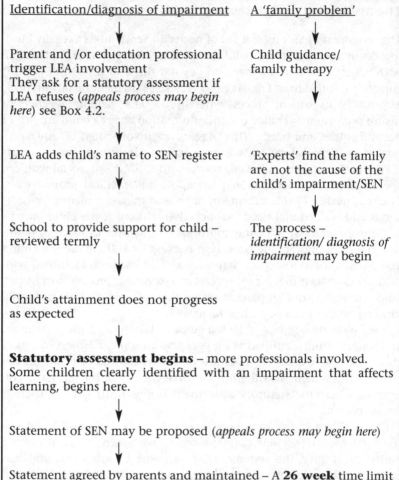

Identification/diagnosis of impairment    A 'family problem'

↓    ↓

Parent and /or education professional    Child guidance/
trigger LEA involvement    family therapy
They ask for a statutory assessment if
LEA refuses (*appeals process may begin*    ↓
*here*) see Box 4.2.

↓

LEA adds child's name to SEN register    'Experts' find the family
are not the cause of the
↓    child's impairment/SEN

↓

School to provide support for child –    The process –
reviewed termly    *identification/ diagnosis of*
*impairment* may begin
↓

Child's attainment does not progress
as expected

↓

**Statutory assessment begins** – more professionals involved.
Some children clearly identified with an impairment that affects
learning, begins here.

↓

Statement of SEN may be proposed (*appeals process may begin here*)

↓

Statement agreed by parents and maintained – A **26 week** time limit
from statutory assessment to agreed statement is laid out in the Code
of Practice (DfES, 2001b), however, if appeals to SEN take place the
time limit is substantially extended

↓

Annual reviews take place with appropriate professionals including
parents

speech and language difficulties and 33 per cent are identified with moderate learning difficulties (ibid.).

In 2004, for the first time, schools in England did submit data on pupils with SEN describing their main need (DfES, 2004a; DfES, 2004b and DfES, 2004c). Of the children with a statement of SEN, 27.8 per cent were classified as having moderate learning difficulties (MLD) and 10.1 per cent with ASD (DfES, 2004c). Detailing the impairment or need may be useful but it would be difficult to place some of the children in this study in particular boxes, as some have more than one impairment, which emphasises the difficulties at the point of diagnosis and assessment. It would be difficult to simply say that *x* number of children have *y* type of difficulty without either elaborating or editing out a less prominent impairment. Significantly, this is also what can make assessing an impaired child difficult as many symptoms of these impairments have similar traits but need different attention when it comes to their education and social learning.

The final stages of the assessment process culminate in the statement of SEN. This is a portfolio of the child and his or her educational needs, as written by education, health, other local authority professionals, as well as the parents, if they 'choose' or are able to contribute. It outlines what provision is needed with the objectives and monitoring structures for meeting those needs. What this means for the provider (in most cases the school) is that the LEA will fund part of that child's support structures, for example, learning support assistants or speech therapist. The statement is a legally binding document; a contract between the LEA, the education provider and, if the parental partnership documents are to be believed, the parents. This is a complicated process and not one case or experience can be described as exactly the same, although similarities are found.

## Some common ground in experiencing the statementing process

All the parents in this study assumed that their child needed a statement of SEN when their child had been diagnosed or identified with SEN. However, not all parents understood the practical implications of this process and document and how it would aid their child throughout their educational career. It does not seem enough for parents to have the LEA suggest that their child can remain within a mainstream school, without specified support recommended in an official document. Parents place an enormous emphasis on 'the statement', as it not only is the child's legal route and right to an appropriate education, it is also a hard copy document that parents can refer to if necessary. Kerry said, 'it [the statement] meant Gary would get a lot of one to one. More support ... especially with speech therapy ... I knew that he would have to have a statement whatever happened ... if he was going to go into a mainstream school'. Parents also spend time and money to justify their child's right to a statement. Trisha's son was born in 1986 and identified with severe dyslexia. He spent from the age of six until he was eight on the LEA's 'stages of need' (now called School Action and School Action Plus). She first had her son privately assessed in London at the age of six years and ten months. This cost £275. Trisha told me, '[i]t took the first year of the juniors ... this was my full-time job. I couldn't do any other work because this was my job'.

Significantly, the statement of SEN is a legally binding document, which once signed can be difficult to change without appeal which is why there is a two month time period to appeal against any part of the statement, for example, the place of education provision stated. Nevertheless, some parents sign it without really understanding the enormity of its implications, as indicated below, especially as this may be during the period of coming to terms emotionally with the identification of an impairment in the first place and then dealing with additional difficulties incurred. For the parents, the statement equals additional support for their child. There can be an assumption and an expectation by the parents that this document will help their child remain in mainstream education. Problems along the way include the class teacher being unable to meet the child's needs, or the educational institution does not always meet the requirements set out by the statement. Katy, whose son, born in 1983 and identified with AS, explained,

> Katy: I think we went through quite a lot of his school life without really knowing what had happened. We seemed to have gone through quite a lot of his school life without actually realising that reports and things ...
> Chrissie: But didn't *you* put in reports?
> Katy: We did but we didn't actually realise what we were doing. We did what we were told, what was asked of us.

If parents do not realise the implications of a statement, they can often feel cheated later on when they find this information out. Katy's husband also suggested that it was not the teachers who were a problem but the EPs and speech therapists, 'all of the people who should have known more about the subject than we did'. It seemed that Katy's husband was disappointed with those professionals and he felt they should have known more about his son's difficulties. Even though Katy's son had a statement they began to realise that what was agreed in the statement was not necessarily being carried out in practice and so began proceedings to appeal for an amendment of the statement.

Una too did not realise what she was signing in the early days. Her son was born in 1983 and assessed with ASD, semantic pragmatic disorder and severe dyspraxia. She was told that he might need a statement when he was five years old. Although she had known there were problems from when he was a baby, due to his developmental delay during routine assessments, Una described her experience in the following way:

> ... so we hit statementing at five and it was suggested that he might need a statement. Nobody had ever spoke to me about this, despite that he would have been entitled to it from two! And his first statement was complete and utter rubbish. I look back on that now ... and I agreed to that! Oh my God! [Laughs].

She was shocked that at the time she agreed to a most inappropriate statement as a result of her preoccupation with the difficulties incurred at the time. Una then spent until her son was eight years old trying to change the statement to suit his needs. These narratives suggest that parents have expectations of what the LEA and the school ought to do. This is due to a growth in discourses around 'partnership' and 'participation' between the school and education delivery and parenting processes (Crozier and Reay, 2004; Vincent, 2000). What the parents' narratives suggest is that there is an unrealistic expectation of what the current LEAs, schools and education professionals can achieve based on official government documents, alongside parents' desire for a solution to the difficulties they face.

Not all the parents interviewed experienced the assessment and statementing process as problematic. Jack, a working class lone father with three sons, two of whom had learning impairments, went through the process with relative ease. (However, there were other problems associated with his younger son's difficulties, but *not* the statementing process). His oldest son's learning difficulties were identified during nursery years and it was suggested by the LEA (in the 1980s) that he went to the local special school. This seemed to prove successful and Jack was pleased with his son's progress. He went to the annual reviews when he could. His other son identified with SEN, five years younger, displayed similar traits, but went to mainstream school. It was discovered during his early years at primary school that he did have some learning difficulties and he was monitored, but the statementing process for him did not begin until late on in junior school. By that point it was suggested to Jack that instead of his son going to mainstream secondary school he should go to the same school as his older brother. Jack was in agreement with this as he felt it was more appropriate. Jack, at the time, had to deal with three young sons and his ex-wife who had deteriorating mental health problems. His sons' educational needs were not at the top of his priorities at that time.

Alternatively, for some middle-class parents, the start of the statementing process called upon their abilities to negotiate with professionals, as Trinny explained.

Because I've had experience of negotiating through my work like for example when the statement came through last summer I looked at it and said 'no way', this is not enough, and I immediately got on to the phone to the child officer and said 'look this isn't good enough' and started negotiating. Maybe I was better placed to because I've got more experience to do that through my work.

However, not all middle class parents undertake this negotiation immediately as highlighted by Una above. Of course every parent has a slightly different story, but the main themes to draw out here are that of emotional and physical energy spent, financial cost and disappointment with the actual intent and proposals of the statement once all assessments have been carried out. The problems incurred are often exacerbated by the fact that the statementing process is an administrative task, yet the emotional energy consumed many parents because it is their child's (dis)abilities, needs *and* humanness mapped out on paper in black and white. Reading and commenting on the statement can be an emotionally draining task in itself as a parent. Not least because the nature of the statement is to highlight problematic areas of need, not to illustrate the flourishing abilities and potential the child may also have. This often leads to conflict between professionals and parents, as illustrated later on in the chapter.

### An assessment and statementing process: biographical reflections

My experience of the assessment process began in about 1995 when I started to collect my own independent data in an attempt to go to the LEA armed with paperwork that 'proved' my daughter needed support. She had an assessment with a psychologist and a speech therapist on 10 August 1995 and a neuro-diagnostic assessment at a 'centre' on

11 September 1995. Both assessments explained that she would need one-to-one educational support. These assessments cost in total about £300. After this initial data gathering I asked my LEA to assess her for a statement, as my daughter was eight years old and in a class of six year olds. The LEA appointed an EP to visit my home and she spent about an hour alone with my daughter. At this time I really had no idea what lay ahead of us and did not anticipate the letter I received from the LEA explaining to me that the EP did not feel that my daughter needed a statutory assessment. I was confused. I knew my daughter had significant learning difficulties as she was not progressing like her peers, and I had the private assessments as proof. I was fortunate to have a friend whose mother gave me advice. She told me to appeal to the LEA for an assessment and use the independent reports. If they refused, then I could start legal proceedings with the SENT. I was scared at the thought of representing my daughter during a legal process.

I need not have concerned myself with going to the tribunal as once the LEA received the letter to begin legal proceedings; they agreed to assess my daughter officially. An EP came to my house and assessed her thoroughly on 1 October 1996. This time I was told that her needs were quite extensive. While I was pleased to be vindicated at last, I felt terribly disappointed and upset that my fears had been realised. The official process of statutory assessment had begun. I received paperwork from the LEA saying that I could write a report about what I thought my daughter's educational and/or emotional needs were. I did this but I had little knowledge of what exactly was expected in this report and was advised by no one. The proposed statement eventually arrived on my doorstep, dated 17 March 1997. The cover letter said: 'I hope that this is now satisfactory to you, but would advise you that you do have the right of appeal to the Special Educational Needs Tribunal. You have two months in which to make an appeal' (Personal document, statement of SEN, 1997). Included in it were the reports I had forwarded and a report from my daughter's school. In Part IV of the statement (placement) it suggested 'This assessment of [my daughter's] special educational needs indicates that she would benefit from placement in a special school catering for pupils with moderate learning difficulties' (ibid.).

I knew this was going to be in the statement because they had already told me, and I had visited two schools for children with MLD and at the time found neither suitable. Instead I chose to educate my daughter at home. However, after over a year out of a school environment I became concerned that my daughter needed her peer group; moreover I was struggling with the boundaries between being mum and teacher, and therefore asked the LEA to reassess with a view to attend mainstream school. Another EP came to see us in March 1998. He was very supportive and made a very thorough assessment, which at my request (and quoting various parts of the updated 'inclusive' policies) recommended that my daughter should be integrated into a mainstream school with a high level of support. I eventually received an amended statement on 13 August 1998 saying in Part IV '[My daughter] should be admitted to [Name], a mainstream secondary school, with effect from September 1998, initially on a part-time basis, building up to full-time' (amended Statement of SEN, 13 August 1998). However, integration into mainstream did not work for my daughter and she never did attend mainstream school full-time again.

This process, from the time my daughter was first referred to the time she received an acceptable statement, spanned six years. Not all of this time was spent proactively working towards the statement, or indeed being thought about, but much emotional, financial and practical energy was invested at various stages during this period. This biographical interlude documents my personal experience of the assessment and statementing process in an attempt to illustrate to the reader a more chronological snapshot of the process.

The following section is not necessarily the norm in the assessment process, but however, is a route to a statement of SEN if the *family* is initially identified as the problem. This is important because if the child is seen to be 'damaged' by the family, his or her educational needs will come second to the family surveillance/needs as a whole, and therefore stifle the educational support that child should have gained.

## A route to assessment: a family problem?

If a child is identified with an impairment that manifests in behavioural or emotional difficulties often the family may be initially blamed or at least assessed, in case of internal familial problems in relationships or parenting methods. In box 4.1 it can be seen that for some families an assessment process may not begin with the assessment of the child, but with the whole family. The actual assessment process has meant that the whole family has initially been placed under surveillance. Rather than the LEA taking the role of provider and supporter of education it can point the finger towards the family, and therefore attempts to 'treat' the family.

### The family as problematic?

Five families in this study were referred to either a child/family clinic or for family therapy, but none of them found this helpful and, in fact, found it traumatic as it was experienced as blame rather than support. These five families had eight children identified with SEN, but at the time of the family consultation recommendation, only one had a statement of SEN. Significantly, the children that have triggered these consultations with professionals have impairments that are *not* easily identifiable, especially early on, and often present with anti-social behaviour, communication difficulties and attention problems. These include AS, AD/HD and severe dyslexia. As said, all of these difficulties can impact on the social maturity and sometimes the behaviour of the child in one way or another, which can be interpreted by others as 'bad parenting'.

Historically, Rose (1989: 159) discusses how 'maladjustment, from bedwetting to delinquency, had become a sign of something wrong in the emotional economy of the family'. Even today there is a risk the family will be questioned if a child behaves outside acceptable social norms. The five mothers describe examples of 'anti-social' behaviour.

Running away from school ... he'd have tables and chairs overturned.

(Marlene)

Running away from school ... self mutilating ... (sighs) forever masturbating and smearing faeces round his room, vomiting, he used to make himself vomit that was all round his bed and on the floor.

(Francis)

He was touching girls in assembly and, erm ... and he didn't seem able to stop it, I mean he didn't rape anybody but ... and then he was saying sexual things to them, so anyway he got suspended.

(Lynne)

He relates to *me* very well, but it's relating to others, that's the problem ... he's so far behind in years it's just ridiculous.

(Debbie)

That night I got called into the school and he'd burnt down two porta-cabins and their contents ... Brad set fire to my house various times ... I used to have a really good babysitter for the other three children ... but once Brad got a little older, eight or nine years old, [the babysitter] was sitting in the chair like that and he came up behind her and held a knife at her throat and said, 'I'm going to fucking kill you' and she wouldn't step foot inside the house again. He's thrown knives at me ... at his brothers ...

(Tracy)

Some parents, teachers, LEA officers and EPs may not consider a child with such behaviour as being 'disabled' with an impairment as such, and therefore look to the family for answers and/or causes. The family comes under the scrutiny of 'new psychological social workers' (Rose, 1989: 159), as can be seen below. Even though a historical account by Rose, still relevant today, considers this kind of behaviour reversible. The family can change the way they behave in order to 'correct' anti-social behaviour. However, these five families would not ordinarily be considered dysfunctional or difficult, in the sense that they were either, middle class and/or economically secure.

Even the most confident of parents can question their mothering abilities though, if their child's behaviour is called into question. It has been argued elsewhere in research on disability, inclusion and choice that '[g]enerally, parents who were able to persuade professionals of the validity of their claims were middle class' (Riddell, 2000: 113). This then may indicate why the mothers in this study either began to question their parenting ability (albeit short lived), clammed up in therapy or found it to be useless.

Debbie was asked to go to a 'family consultation meeting' after she had suggested to a professional (within the school medical service) that her son might have AS. From looking at her story it seemed clear that the meeting was about trying to establish any problem areas in the family or a history of AS symptoms, before diagnosing anything else. If I were to go to the doctor with a heart problem I would understandably be asked about my family history. This way of eliminating or confirming family and/or genetic links to an impairment may be fine for the professionals, but the emotional vulnerability of the mother and/or the father (already discussed in the previous chapter) make questions about them as a family unit particularly traumatic. As Debbie recalled,

> I thought they're going to think I'm a terrible mother, obviously needs to be taken into care [Laughs]. ... The whole family went [two adults and two children]. She [the psychologist] asked [my son] about school and various things and she asked us about our families, and were our parents still alive, and what we thought of the school ... when we went to school, have we got brothers and sisters, who were we closest to...? At the end of the day I said to her, 'had I got good reason to be here?' I'm so fed up with being looked down upon as a neurotic mother.

Debbie's son refused to do certain things in the meeting, like go into the corner of the room and draw his family, and Debbie said, 'and at the end they asked if he would like to see someone special he could talk to and relate to and he said, "yes". Actually, when it came to it, they said they had "no one to do the job", as they never filled the empty vacancy'. It is significant here that there arc a group of professionals who look at the child's behaviour and attempt to analyse it in relation to the *whole family* to eradicate the link between the 'bad parent' and 'difficult child', but in this case it seemed that once it had been established the family was *not* the cause of the child's difficulties no family therapy was therefore required and the child and family were then left to wait for intervention and support via the education route.

### Apportioning blame: a middle class story

Francis, whose son Mark, aged 12, had been diagnosed with AD/HD and AS, told me he did not have a statement (at the time of interview) as he was in the process of being assessed. It was the 'school that called in the family consultation unit' assuming that something was 'not quite right' at home. The whole family (mother, father, three children and the au pair) were asked to attend, and Francis said that it was the only time she had taken her other two children to any meeting related to Mark. Their experience of it was short but memorable.

The family consultation unit was an absolute disaster ... we were slated ... as a family. We had lack of continuity of support at home because we had au pairs, and me working, and we had [my husband] who came over dreadfully. He can't handle anything like that. I mean he was gazing at the ceiling and I thought 'shit we're just being hung here'. I was still in my uniform [nurse] because one of my clinics had run late which went down a hoot, and I staggered in with my briefcase and Mark was under the chair and round the room, [my daughter] wouldn't talk at all ... it was just before she went on anti depressants and she resented being there and said, 'there's nothing wrong with me' ... and he [her oldest son] was laughing manically because Mark was so awful, so [her oldest son] is laughing and thinking, 'what the hell are we doing here', and I just winked at him, we're on the same wavelength, and I could see this is bad news and I thought, 'oh well what the hell', and they started on about Mark and 'are his symptoms relieved when his bowels are opened?' [She breaks down laughing]. And [her husband] who's on another planet anyway, has never come across anything psychiatric in his life ever, never, and thought, 'what on earth's going on?' He got lost on that and said, 'how does having your bowels open ... how does that help us in here?' And he got very agitated ... 'to listen to this crap', which didn't go down very well because as far as the professionals were concerned, he [my husband] wasn't open-minded and willing to help and change and move on ... we came out of there *us* needing 'intensive family support work', I mean everything. You name it ... we had a whole list, I said 'get stuffed! You'll never see me cross your doorstep again'. And so that, according to the professionals, was 'objectionable, un-cooperating.... Blah, blah blah', back to us again, the family. So I went back to the hospital and said, 'if you ever put us through that again you can get stuffed as well ...' it's an insult that you sent us to a place like that'.

It is clear from this detailed excerpt that Francis and her family were very uncomfortable with this whole situation of being surveyed, even though they may have come across, to the professionals, as difficult and uncooperative, because as far as the professionals were concerned they were asking appropriate questions. However, all the family wanted was support and help with their son. They did not realise that they might be blamed, or at the very least, feel blamed for their son's difficult behaviour.

The professionals had an agenda (to find out if there were any problems in the family, and see if they could support them), and the family, by being viewed as uncooperative, were assigned the label of a 'dysfunctional family' who needed 'intensive family support work'. It is argued that the parents, especially the mother, stand as mediators between the private world of the family and the public (Crozier and Reay, 2004; Read, 2000; Vincent, 2000). This involves the regulation of the child's social, moral and intellectual well-being (Vincent, 2000; Walkerdine and Lucey, 1989). It is hardly surprising then the impact of being told, or made to feel, that a mother and indeed family are not doing the 'job' properly is immense. Especially when the emotional angst of what has been (and may still be) going on (as described in the previous chapter). Significantly, out of the five families, in this study, the two working class mothers were desperate for help, and wanted the involvement of the professionals, but Marlene's husband would never turn up to the meetings and Tracy wanted respite rather than counselling. The middle class mothers seemed to feel an increased intensity of blame.

Lynne had a similar experience to Francis where she felt she was made to feel she had in some way damaged her son, Kevin. The statementing process did not start until he was 14 years old and yet at 11 years she had been told he had a low IQ (often children diagnosed with AS have a high IQ but this is not always the case), but no support at that time was forthcoming. In fact after her son was suspended for inappropriate behaviour with girls at school, he was referred to the child and family guidance clinic at the age of 13. Lynne was relieved because she thought finally someone was going to help. There was a time when she and her partner, as well as her son went to the clinic, but unlike Francis, it was suggested they were seen separately, as Lynne explained,

> I was assigned to a senior social worker and he, Kevin, was assigned to this other woman, and it was all a bit weird ... Kevin said, 'I can't stand going and I'm not going any more' ... he could not talk about himself, and still can't. So he sat there in silence. Then they started getting out these boxes to help him talk and that didn't work. ... He wasn't doing his work, but then I used to see this senior social worker and that ... in the end I think I said something like, 'why am I here? What is the point of this?' and he said, 'well we work on the assumption that you have damaged your child emotionally ...' 'WHAT ?' ... 'and that's how child and family guidance clinics work?!' 'Yes'. That is the premise that they work on, that the family has damaged the child. And I just sat there, 'but he was ... but he was born like it ... you know he's had special needs since the day he was born! There's something wrong with *him*'.

Lynne was desperate to be told as a mother that she was not at fault and indeed suggested she knew this to be the case. After Kevin was diagnosed initially with pervasive developmental disorder (PDD), commonly known as childhood autism, she recalled, '... I felt vindicated. I felt that I could turn round and tell them all to get stuffed then'. This diagnosis of impairment stripped away any lingering doubts about her own poor parenting, as well as confirming what she already believed to be true.

## A working class alternative?

Tracy, a working class mother with four sons (two with impairments), had a different story to tell. Her youngest son, Brad, was diagnosed with a rare syndrome at the age of nine (that presented with significant anti-social behaviour), but before this diagnosis she had little support even though his behaviour was clearly disrupting the whole family. One time she called the social services as a cry for help, but

> they told me they were too busy to do anything. So I said, 'so basically I've got to kick the shit out of my child before you do anything?' and the bloke on the phone said, 'unfortunate as that is, yes'. I said, 'don't bloody tempt me, I'm that far from doing it'. I was. ... there

were times when I'd sit there and I'd be like that gritting my teeth ... I hated him ... I loved him, but I hated him. I really detested him, the child he was, and what he did. I was in tears all the time, erm ... his brothers were never happy, they hated him ... finally I'd been to the doctors and ... and we got sent to a family and child consultation clinic. Erm ... and they were about as much use as a chocolate fireguard really ... they gave him some medication.

Tracy was desperate for some respite from the difficulties that she faced and yet was met with resistance initially. But even when she did receive some support said they were of no use, as it was not therapy that was needed, but support and respite.

## In discussion

It seems that all the parents want support, but do not know how to get it, and are frequently in a highly emotional state by the time they deal with the professional services. This often leads them to behave in ways that do not 'fit in' with culturally or socially accepted norms: to love your child regardless, and to cope with childcare and mothering practices. If this behaviour is apparent, outside agencies often assume that rather than the child causing the mother and family to become distressed and difficult, the lack of mother's love or a dysfunctional family has caused the child's problems. Hollway and Featherstone (1997), Parker (1997) and Ribbens (1994) refer to maternal ambivalence and see this as a part of ordinary motherhood. Yet the 'complex and contradictory state of mind, shared variously by all mothers, in which loving and hating feelings for children exist side by side' (Parker, 1997: 17) may seem culturally unacceptable and when it is revealed by the frustrated mother, the consequences can seem harsh. What about the mother with a child who behaves in socially unacceptable ways? Can one expect these feelings to be heightened? As seen above, the results can be emotionally traumatic for the whole family and many of the mothers have expressed some kind of maternal ambivalence or despair. Kerry has been sterilised rather than have another impaired child. Marlene said that she would not have had children if she had known what it would be like. And out of the 25 children, in this research, over the age of six, nine are attending/have attended residential specialist provision. For example, Una and Francis said they could not cope with their sons at home, indicating a difficulty hard to cope with on a day-to-day basis.

Discussing delinquency, Donzelot (1979: 97) says that 'experts in criminology' peel away the layers of the 'delinquent's past', and as has occurred with the above examples, an attempt is being made to discover the route of the difficulty, especially as they often manifest in behavioural difficulties. And Walkerdine, discussed by Wyness, argues,

> [t]he idea of a maternal responsibility suggests that mothers are held accountable for their children because of a middle-class model of 'normal' development that filters through the schools. A pathology of inadequate socialisation is constructed through this covert regulation in class that implicated working-class mothers by encouraging them to believe that they are responsible for their children's failings.
>
> (Wyness, 1996: 11)

Here though I am not able to say there is a distinction between the child's identified impairments and the socio-economic group the children come from. The children have behaviour that has commonly been described as difficult and unruly, and yet the parents argue they have successfully parented their other children without impairments. Debbie insisted, 'My other son is fine, is a pleasure'. Moreover, increased 'family blame' might emerge if there is more than one child with difficulties. Marlene has three sons with impairments and Francis's older daughter did not talk for the first few years of her life.

It is a significant and telling point that the five families referred for family therapy were not among those children statemented in the early years, and in fact, had children whose impairments included anti-social behaviour. For these families, the assessment process mapped out above has been a messy and traumatic process that came *before* an official identification of impairment and assessment of SEN. It was also experienced as a problematic relationship between the professionals and themselves. As the chapter unfolds, the reader will discover that for Lynne the process has been ongoing from birth to post 16, and for Francis the LEA did not begin a statutory assessment of her son until the age of 12. It is important to emphasise what has been discussed is only the beginning for some families; the actual statementing process had not begun until the family were discounted as part of the problem. The following section documents the appeals process and legal battles with a closer look at two parents' stories.

## Legal dilemmas

In this section I illustrate, with two stories, the legal battles that can take place when parents realise the statement of SEN has not been carried out as appropriately. Because the statement of SEN is a legally binding document, making changes can be a difficult process. All parents go into this process not as an expert in the education of their child, but in the first instance, as a mother or father. As described, parents can often sign the statement before they realise the legal implications of such a document. As parents become aware of their child's impairment and future needs they often realise that their child has a right to support not specified in the statement, or that the education professionals are not carrying out the identified support. In general, historically it has been argued that middle class parents have taken more of an interest in their children's education than working class parents (Douglas, 1964). However, while there may be differences in *how* parents negotiate the education system, the class distinction is not simply one of working or middle class, non-involvement or involvement, lack of interest or interest, respectively (David et al., 1993; Reay, 1998; Vincent, 2000).

Over half of the parents in this study appealed to the LEA or SENT against aspects of their child's statement, or appealed for their child to be assessed. Two of these parents have gone through the whole legal process ending up at the High Court or very close to it. In Tina's case the LEA backed down after receiving the High Court papers, albeit reluctantly, and Lynne won a High Court appeal. Parents are expected to be present at the SENT and usually represent themselves, but in some cases parents will have either a barrister or an independent representative from the voluntary sector if they are unable to, or do not want to represent themselves, for whatever reason. Tina and Lynne are middle class and were able to finance the necessary private reports and assessments, as well as having the cultural capital to negotiate this process. Other parents in this research, for example Francis and Trisha, have spent hundreds, if not thousands of pounds on reports, assessments and tuition. (Trisha and her husband re-mortgaged their house to find the money and Francis's husband worked abroad for a higher income). The pressure on families to provide 'evidence' of their case is clear and therefore a drain on financial resources and can cause deep emotional stress.

The fundamental points seem to be, the parents' cultural confidence (to negotiate with professionals) and their economic security (to be able to pay for assessments and legal advice and support). For example, Trisha, a working class mother with moderate family income, was able to re-mortgage her house to pay school fees while she was in conflict with the LEA about a specialist out of county residential placement. Before moving on to two middle class parents' stories I want to ask whether the changes in the policy over the past decade have simplified the process of assessment and statementing?

## Caught in the Act

Since the Education Act 1993 there have been a few changes with regard to the statementing process, as highlighted by Docking (2000: 108).

- There are limits over how long each stage takes now.
- The 1993 Act required the Secretary of State to issue a Code of Practice on the identification and assessment of children with SEN that would act as a guidance manual for LEAs and the schools. This Code came out in 1994 but has now been revised and the new Code was implemented in January 2002. This is not a legal document like the Acts, however the government *expects* that LEAs and schools adhere to its recommendations.
- It extended the rights of parents to appeal against LEA decisions with regard to assessing, statementing and maintaining a statement in creating independent SENT to hear appeals.

This latter point has had an effect on parents and their rights with regard to their impaired child. Not only have parents taken it upon themselves to represent their case against a LEA at the SEN and disability tribunal when a decision has been made they may disagree with it. Voluntary organisations have also emerged in an attempt to advocate for those parents unable to represent themselves. The new policies have not made it a simpler process, however with the extended rights of parents, and the independent SENT there are legal procedures parents can follow even if it is a difficult process. Reasons for appealing to the SENT vary and can be based on whether a child needs a statement or not, or if a statement is given what provision or type of school is named. It could be that a special school or mainstream school is indicated and the parents disagree with the proposed type of school, depending on whether they want their child to be included in mainstream education or educated in a school that has specific facilities or services their child requires.

I highlight this legal process by illustrating two middle class mothers' stories. They have appealed their child's statement of SEN not only to the SENT but also to the High Court. As Friel (1997: 123) says, '[a]n appeal to the High Court is highly technical and should not be conducted by just any lawyer. As time is of the essence, an experienced solicitor should be consulted on receipt of a decision'. This eliminates many of the parents who would be economically vulnerable or culturally removed from the legal system. Box 4.2 describes the appeals process that parents have to go through if they 'choose' to appeal against a decision made by the LEA or education providers.

### Box 4.2 The appeals process

Parents can appeal to the SENT for various reasons, the main ones being:

- If the parents, health professional, teacher, SENCO or nursery staff ask the LEA to assess for a statement and they refuse,
- If the LEA is asked to amend the statement but refuses,
- If the parents or teachers feel the statement of SEN is not adequate to meet the child's SEN. (They have two months to appeal from when the statement is proposed).

Once the LEA has issued the SENT date they may then begin *the process of assessment* and ask the parent to withdraw from the SENT.

**OR** the LEA may decide to go to the SENT. In this case the parents then have to gather evidence to prove the child needs an assessment or that the statement is inadequate. Parents may represent themselves at court or have an advocate. The evidence would usually be a professional report, for example, from an EP or speech therapist who is in agreement with the parents' demands. The SENT board includes a chairperson (usually a lawyer) and two other SEN 'experts'.

If the LEA wins the case they do not have to do anything, the parents have to accept the statement as it is proposed.

**OR** the parents can take the LEA or SENT to High Court.

If the parents win the case the LEA will be asked to begin a statutory assessment or amend the proposed statement as suggested by the SENT. *The assessment process may begin here.*

If the parents get the High Court to issue a writ, the LEA will be notified. (At this point the LEA may begin the *assessment process* or make necessary changes to the statement).

The parents will need legal representation and more evidence to prove why the decisions made at the SENT were wrong. If the parents win the High Court case then the *assessment process begins here*, OR changes to the statement are made, OR the parents return back to the SENT for another hearing.

**From beginning to end, such a process can take years, if at each stage there are conflicts of opinions and objectives between the LEA and parents, for example.**

### Tina's tribunal story

Tina is a middle class mother with three children: a 13-year-old son and seven-year-old twin daughters, one of whom (Teresa) has a speech and language impairment and dyspraxia. This story is one where Tina not only had to deal with her own emotions but also spent two years in conflict with her husband (the father of her children). She explained,

> gradually you come to terms with the difficulties realising that you've got to get up and fight for the provisions they need and this takes about two years and at the end of that two years they've [her husband in this case] probably taken it on board, although the pain never goes away altogether, and the fathers' are possibly just beginning to acknowledge there's a problem.

This illustrates how Tina perceives the difference in how she and her husband have come to terms with the difficulties thus far. Upon realising that her daughter had more significant problems than she initially assumed, she decided to go to a conference for parents of children with SEN, and took along her daughter's statement of SEN. It was heavily criticised by one of the workshop leaders and Tina was told that Teresa really should be in a speech and language unit, not in mainstream school, where the provision was not appropriate. 'I was so taken aback by this because I was still imagining Teresa to be in mainstream. For someone to say specialist provision, is another major shock'. A growing number of voluntary organisations have become an important source of support and advice for parents of children with SEN (Carpenter, 2000; Miller, 2000; Vincent, 2000). Tina found the conferences and voluntary organisations to be an invaluable support; especially as her domestic support structures were fragile.

Tina felt she had no support at the time, from home, and in fact experienced negative responses rather than no response, as in some cases.

> I was on the floor for about three months, just taken aback at the idea of a language unit and [the speech therapist] told me you've got to get your head around it and get up and fight, but my husband was saying 'I think she'll be fine at the mainstream school, I don't know why she needs speech therapy because it wasn't in the statement, clearly you know all this is a load of neurotic women talking a load of mumbo jumbo, and I know best'.

The tension between Tina and her husband only got worse during this period and she was torn as she indicated here, 'these people were saying get up and fight'. Her husband said, 'oh she'll be alright'. Tina though told me, she replied, 'I'm not having you ruin Teresa's education ... I believe these people know what they are talking about' ... I told him what I was doing and he didn't agree with me and I just said, 'I'm doing it!' [She laughed] 'I don't care what you say'. Tina told the LEA that she was taking them to the SENT for speech therapy and placement changes in the statement. She got a solicitor (although parents do not need one) and then paid for an independent EP report.

Tina revealed that her husband was still unsympathetic, but he did say that he thought she would know the case of his daughter more than any barrister, but Tina did not feel she could represent herself and explained, 'I felt that because it was my child I was so emotionally involved I was worried I might freeze on the day and be unable to talk'. Tina's husband did go to the tribunal with her and it lasted about four hours. The tribunal found in favour of Teresa and suggested a language unit, but the LEA did not issue the new statement and there was a furore. Tina eventually decided that she would need to go to the High Court to get the provision the SENT had proposed. Teresa had already started the mainstream school with her twin sister and was not getting the support she needed.

Tina's LEA was issued with a High Court writ. It was at this point the LEA backed down and chose to adhere to the tribunal suggestions. If they had lost it would have cost between £50,000 and £100,000 in legal costs. All of this took its toll on Tina, who was by then on beta-blockers for panic attacks. Her husband continued to say that sending their daughter to the language unit would 'cause Teresa great psychological damage'. Tina and her husband spent a huge amount of money on this whole process and she told me, 'if you can't afford the professional reports then you've got to rely on the LEA ones, so you're stuck really. You've got to be able to afford professional reports and representation if you want it'. The tribunal cost them about £4000. It had taken about two years for her husband to come round to thinking that she was doing the right thing and she told me, 'he's coming to recognise the extent of problems', to the point that they are now looking into out of county residential provision. This case indicates how much pressure may be put onto a relationship when the assessment process becomes a legal battleground, in addition to the emotions of discovering and dealing with difference.

### Lynne's tribunal story

Lynne's story differs from Tina's in that she did go to High Court, and that unlike Tina her partner (not Kevin's father) was very supportive. Lynne too is middle class, divorced, and has an 18-year-old son Kevin, who had been diagnosed with AS and epilepsy. She separated from his father when Kevin was three years old and told me it was because 'he [her partner] was on the outside, it was me and the baby'. She now lives with the father of her second son. Kevin had trouble from the moment he started school, as illustrated below. He went to mainstream primary and secondary until the age of 14. Lynne was constantly asking the LEA for him to be assessed for a statement, but had never appealed at that time. He was suspended from school for inappropriate sexual behaviour and then spent a year in home tuition. Lynne felt that he needed specialist education but the 'LEA tried to persuade us to go back into mainstream ... I couldn't believe it!' Eventually at the age of 14, Kevin was diagnosed with PDD (a name for childhood autism), but even then it was not a smooth path. Lynne could not make it to the meeting where a board of professionals decided whether or not to begin a statutory assessment for a statement because she was in hospital, but her partner attended in her place. Lynne explained that her partner

> got them [the LEA] to agree to it! And it was almost like I'd been at meetings they'd never taken any notice of me ... and then there's a man and they take notice of him, who's also not his father, but in that parent role.

Here Lynne implies that those professionals involved in the meeting had previously undermined her status as a mother, so much so, that her partner, an educated man and not her son's father (although acting in the parental role) was in a more powerful position than the biological father or the mother.

After it had been agreed that a special school would be appropriate, Kevin was nevertheless turned away from two schools for children with MLD. She told me one of the head teachers 'didn't show us around and he said ... he got a directory of schools off the shelf and he gave it to us and said, "would you like to borrow that? Send your son to one of those"'. They went to see another MLD school and were told there was not a place for Kevin. He was finally accepted into the only one left in her geographical area. From that time, Kevin progressed more rapidly. It was then that Lynne began to think about post-16 specialist education. Knowing there was little provision in her local area she began to look out of county. Like Tina, Lynne made use of a local voluntary organisation: an AS support group. She had spoken to other parents and was told that if she wanted an out of county placement she would need to start doing research long before her son reached 16. 'I naively thought the

LEA would find a place', she said. She then started her quest to find a suitable college and told me, 'you have to go round and look at them and find the one for you. [Gasps] What a lot of work!' She did find one that she considered appropriate, but she also made it clear that she had to 'play a game'. 'I also wanted to play on the fact that he had epilepsy to get him an out of county placement'. This is because the LEA would not fund a place unless there is unsuitable provision in county. The problem is that often the out of county college/school may not *offer* provision unless there is a guarantee of funding from the LEA.

To try to prove the college she had chosen was the most appropriate for her son, Lynne had to provide the LEA with professional reports spelling out the reasons for a residential placement. By this time she was on an autistic national mailing list and she had noticed a psychologist who was 'spot on, very good', in answering parents' questions. Significantly, even Lynne realised her financial situation had made a difference, as highlighted here as she said it cost

> about £300 ... so then I got my little bundle together ready to fight the LEA and erm ... 'cause he had kindly written that he needed to go to a specialist college [laughs], yes I suppose if you've got the money and you get the right person you are paying for that person to write the thing that you want them to write. But that's life.

However, this was only the beginning of the financial and emotional implications for Lynne.

The psychologist had also warned her that the LEA would not inform her before the statement ceased and if she wanted post-16 education and the statement to continue she would need to put this in writing before he left school.

> So I wrote to the LEA saying that, 'I understand you will be stopping my son's statement at the end of this term. Please would you confirm this in writing and give me' ... the psychologist told me what to say ... . 'under the education act such and such a date to erm ... appeal against this' ... so they had to do that, once you've done that, so a letter came back saying 'yes they were going to stop his statement and this is what I do if I wish to appeal'. That's the magic piece of paper, once you've got that you can appeal, but it's getting that. Most parents think that they automatically get that letter and they don't. So it's really nasty stuff.

Lynne put in her appeal to the LEA but received a letter back from the SENT saying they would not hear her case because her son was no longer on a school register. Lynne had put in her appeal *before* Kevin left school, but the LEA had not sent her the letter of appeal until after her son had left school. She sought legal advice from a voluntary organisation and they advised her to get a specialist lawyer. Lynne claimed disability living allowance (DLA) and severe disability allowance (SDA) for her son, but saved this for the legal fees, which ran into several thousand pounds. 'I got legal aid for the first part of the process because that's in Kevin's name and then the next part wasn't and I couldn't get legal aid ...' She took the SENT to High Court on the grounds that the 'spirit of the act had been contravened'.

This was an emotional and time-consuming period, and Lynne felt she was

> public enemy number one with everybody then. Special educational needs tribunal didn't like me [laughs] because I was taking them to court, and you know they're supposed to be on the side of kids with special needs so ... I suppose they don't like being taken to court, nobody does. And erm ... and I was obviously public enemy number one with my LEA, because they were co- defendant, I can't remember quite why now, but I've got a filing cabinet of all the documents, so they had to attend court as well, and there was a judge and everything, it took quite a long time, it took two days ... I suppose it came down in the end that it was the maladministration of the LEA ... I think they turned up the first day and didn't turn up the second day.... We won the case; the judge ordered that the special educational needs tribunal had to hear the case. So we then had to go to the tribunal!

The tribunal case was difficult because one of Kevin's teachers was there on the opposing side saying that he did not need specialist provision, but eventually they found in Tina's favour. However, the story does not end there, as the LEA tried to get Kevin into a specialist college *in the county*. Lynne and her partner did more 'research' and found the office of standards in education (OFSTED) report for this college uncomplimentary and unsatisfactory. Her partner knew someone who had done some transport work for the LEA and he found out how much it would cost the LEA for the college and transport to the 'in county' college and then went to speak to an education officer and said,

> 'Everything is driven by money isn't it?' And she said, 'well no, everything is driven by the best interest of the child'. I said, 'everything is driven by money, in the name of the interest of the child'

and she was a bit quiet at that, and I said, 'look how's this for a proposition'?'

They procured the place out of county for Kevin on the proviso that Lynne, or her husband, would transport him there and back, which would reduce the transport budget for the LEA.

There is both an economic and cultural vulnerability involved here when taking either an LEA or SENT to High Court. While many working class mothers do take an active interest in their children's education (Crozier and Reay, 2004; Reay, 1998; Vincent, 2000), they may not be able to negotiate the cultural agendas or have the finances to cover the costs in dealing with these difficulties. It is clear from these stories that the mothers became the advocates for their children, even if in the final stages they did 'buy in' expert support. For example, coming into conflict with the LEA or SENT is not the norm for parents with impaired children, but it does happen, and if more parents were informed about the statement of SEN and its implications early on, there might be more appeals. This is contrary to what public policy suggests with the rhetoric of partnership between parents and professionals. The following section unpacks this conflict with direct reference to problematic relationships between professionals and parents.

## Parents and 'partnership'

New Labour and their government have published social policies and directives on 'partnerships' and promoted it as a term and practice to adhere to (Glendinning et al., 2002).

> Like 'community', partnership is a word of obvious virtue '[what sensible person would choose conflict over collaboration]?' [...] Despite their wide variations in organisational and social relationships, processes and arrangements, partnerships provide a key, overarching and unifying imagery of this Third Way approach to governing.
>
> (Clarke and Glendinning, 2002: 33)

Policies on education have not been excluded within this discourse and yet interpretations of what partnership means in practice can often be far removed from comfortable notions of 'joined-up working' and 'togetherness'. During the assessment process and beyond there is an assumption that parents will be involved in some kind of partnership with the professionals involved. 'Partnership with parents plays a key role in promoting a culture of co-operation between parents, schools, LEAs and others' (DfES, 2001a: 2:1). The policy also specifies that parents are experts in their field and that 'Parents hold key information and have a critical role to play in their children's education' (ibid.). Not unsurprisingly then, parents expect a level of partnership and are disappointed when often their cries for help, support, and their lay diagnoses either come up against official indifference or initiate conflict when they approach health or education professionals.

All 24 of the parents, irrespective of their class position, have at some point described this process as a fight or battle with different professionals in powerful positions, as illustrated here,

> He does deserve this care, but we can't provide it, but we'll keep fighting ... we will keep fighting.
>
> (Neil)

> I feel like it's a one man battle and if you're not there behind your child checking out all the options, working overtime, then they'll just pass you by because nobody really cares that much.
>
> (Kim)

> We actually have to have a fight on our hands, I mean you only have to look at the whole history to realise that's what we do and life's a struggle, but you may not want to have that particular fight because you expect that service [the LEA] to do that.
>
> (Una)

> I had no choice. It was against my wishes, because I always believed that all I had to do was keep fighting and find another school and it would become what I wanted.
>
> (Karen)

> I keep fighting ... I can't give up and on one hand I'm saying I don't want him, take him away and on the other hand I grab him and can't switch off and can't stop ... if I'm not writing official letters, I'm reading about new education law ...
>
> (Brenda)

What is clear from these quotes, and throughout this following section, is that although policymakers claim there is a partnership between parents and professionals during the assessment and statementing process, the relationship is rarely experienced as such. Vincent (2000: 40) in her research claims that 'The language used in both local and national documents is consensual, minimizing conflict and emphasising "partnership"'. However, she suggests there are contradictions, between policymakers encouraging parents to come forward and appeal decisions made by the LEA, and the actual lack of registrations of appeals made. This means that although the promotion of choice and legal appeal is encouraged there are more parents who do not appeal.

The investment of time and energy both practically and emotionally is immense, and may bear no relevance to class. However, differences may emerge in the way the parents negotiate the system, reactions from the professionals, and therefore the outcomes for both the parents and their child. As Diane Reay points out in her research on class, education and mothers,

> [a]lthough many of the working class women had fewer cultural resources than middle class mothers, including far lower incomes, fewer educational qualifications, less educational knowledge and information about the system, this did not indicate lower levels of involvement in children's education. What it did mean was less effective practices, as working class women found it difficult to assume the role of the educational expert, were less likely to persuade the teachers to act on their complaints and were ill-equipped financially, socially and psychologically to compensate for the deficits they perceived in their children's education.
>
> (1998: 163)

### 'It's a ton weight': dealing with professionals in their numbers

One of the main features of parenting an impaired child with SEN is the number of professionals involved in the child's life. A child without impairments could ordinarily have professionals such as a dentist, GP, teachers, and possibly an optician, involved in his or her life. With my daughter the list looked nothing like that. At one time the number of professionals I personally had to deal with included an orthodontist (brace work for her tongue thrust), physiotherapist, paediatrician, osteopath, EP, neuro-physiological psychologist, orthopaedic specialist, speech therapist, education officer, SENCO, learning support assistants, voluntary advisors, private tutors, and these are just the ones I remember! All of these professionals had something different to say, and some gave me 'homework' to do with my daughter. Significantly, all the professionals 'involved' in the parents' lives have a slightly different story to dictate regarding the child's difficulties, they all have a piece of the parents' life, which can at times be overwhelming at the very least.

Russell (1997: 79) found in her research on families with severely impaired children, that one family noted,

> Some of us families collect professionals like other people collect stamps. But knowing 17 different professionals isn't partnership. It's a survival exercise with often conflicting advice, everyone with expectations and a bag of homework at the end of the day that makes you feel you should be the real professionals!

As highlighted, it would probably be difficult to partner all the professionals involved. Una described her presentation to parents in her professional capacity as a helpline manager.

> On one of the overheads, I have this ton weight with 123 professionals, and that's what it is, and then you talk to the audience and they say 'God yeah'. And if you've got a child with more than one disability you start over again, all these people you have to engage with. In [my sons] case he was picked up at two. ... At last tot up and the end of the last academic year it was 111. We since then moved into another academic year and into careers services. I think there's now about 120?

Braun (2001) on parenting perspectives suggests, mothers may feel trapped because on one hand they want to take care of their children without public support (be 'good' mothers), and on the other hand they need or want specialist support. Babs explained about her experience of professional involvement.

> The next minute he was being taken over by all these things that we had to go and do ... lengthy interviews with speech and language ... it was partly investigative too. ... I hated everyday I went to that place [play therapy in a specialist playgroup]. I hated every time I took him. I felt deeply humiliated somehow.

Parents are often in a quandary between wanting to take charge and feeling totally out of control and awash with professionals. Kerry, with regard to decision-making with professionals, quite categorically stated that

> I feel it's really important that parents take part in what decision is going to be made for the child ... this is going to effect him for the rest of his life, you know, those decisions. I think that although

they're very professional people and they will do their best for him, from what I've seen so far ... I've been to the school reviews, there were situations that came up where I felt they didn't actually know Gary how I knew him.

Kerry at this point said she had the confidence to voice her opinions at these meetings, although she did tell me that she would often have to fight back the tears. It is clear from these narratives that parental partnership is difficult to obtain given the sheer numbers of professionals involved in the parents' lives.

### Dealing with difficulty: parental 'absence'

In the second interview with Marlene we discussed a review meeting and she handed me the minutes, which I read out:

> Chrissie: So in this report from last month it's got here the professionals attending the meeting were: ed psych, teacher, speech therapist, child psychiatrist, doctors and student, the head teacher, SENCO, class teacher, health visitor ... all those people?! Were you at this meeting?
>
> Marlene: Yeah, I was there as well. I don't know why I don't get a mention [laughs].

I continued to read out the minutes:

> Chrissie: Janet, 'unable to attend'. Who's that?
>
> Marlene: She's the 'parent in partnership' officer!

Not only were there 11 people at the meeting, Marlene was there as the only 'non professional'. There was no parent partnership representative present and she did not even get a mention in the meetings' minutes. Her exclusion from this administrative record seems symbolic of the lack of partnership. It could be that there was already a set agenda to this meeting and the actual meeting took place as a practical and administrative task rather than a 'real' space for discussion and negotiation which would account for Marlene's 'absence'.

Katy's husband told of a less symbolic absence. 'They [the LEA] sent a letter about the parent partnership steering group meeting, and then said they weren't having any parents on the steering group partnership, which I thought was very strange'. For Foucault (1973) in an explanation of the 'medical gaze' and Culpitt (1999: 144) the 'welfare gaze', as the latter explains, '[t]he looking was not so much a discovery but a confirmation, an attempt to prove what was already known'. Culpitt explains that by virtue of claiming welfare, a person is known as dependent, and that 'to seek public support is to define yourself as needy, and by definition dependent' (1999: 144). The same can be said for those parents of impaired children with SEN. The parents are looking for solutions to problems, and the professionals are often working within a set bureaucratic and state/discipline led agenda, which does not necessarily include the parents' important and relevant knowledge. Yet this emotional and practical knowledge may be an important part of the puzzle when attempting to put together a package of support for a child. Moreover, parents need to feel party to this process in dealing with this difficulty.

### Parental knowledge, expert knowledge: unequal status?

There seems to be an unequal distribution of status between the parents and professionals. So much so that partnership can be difficult to negotiate. To emphasise the parental knowledge, here are some examples from this study commenting on situations when parents have attempted to interact with professionals, imparting their knowledge. Kerry revealed about talking with her sons paediatrician,

> 'Oh yes he's probably epileptic and I'm going to put him on Epilim' [the paediatrician said]. Whether he thought I was going to take that I don't know, but he didn't even lift his face up when talking to me ... he was writing and he didn't even look up ... I had to go up and put my face right under his face and say to him, 'excuse me but could you have the decency to look a me when you're talking to me when discussing my child'. And from that moment on he was fine, he respected me more because I asked lots of questions.

Kerry like others have commented on a less than equal status when it comes to dealing with the professionals, for example, Neil stressed,

> again as a parent been told basically ... patted on the head, patted on the head by the speech therapist, 'you know, oh well, you're a parent, you're bound to over react under these sorts of circumstances', and bollocks am I over reacting. I know my son, I know certain things, he may be a so-called expert but I know certain things as well.

Significantly, the dismissive attitudes towards the parents are not exclusive to the mothers. Neil felt patronised and angry about how he was treated, as highlighted above, and assumed to be too emotionally involved to have any objectivity about his son's difficulties. Again the question of knowing their child more than the professionals seems to take precedence over any professional statement, and yet the parents yearned for some answers. The parents may be asking for advice, and trying to gain knowledge from the professionals, without success. Katy's husband, when talking about his experience of trying to find out about AS, said,

> we were a little disappointed because the stage we went through, we were looking to the 'so called' professionals and experts to give us guidance, and to tell us what was going on, and you realise they were in the dark in some ways, as much as we were ... it turned out that we knew more about the subject than some of them! They should *know* about it not just have heard about it.

Trinny was surprised at how impenetrable the language was when talking to an EP and how disappointed she was when she did not get straight answers to her son's problems.

> He was difficult to understand and I'm reasonably articulate and I found him difficult to understand. ... You know there were times when I had to stop and say look you need, erm, it wasn't someone who came out speaking plain English.

There are not always straightforward answers with regard to many of the children's impairments within my research, and yet it seems important for parents to know what is going on and how to deal with it.

To return to Culpitt's (1999) point about seeking public (or specialist knowledge); the parent here is forced into a cruel dependency transferred to them by virtue of having an impaired child. I say cruel at this point because the emotional experience is often painful and at times humiliating. Culpitt goes on to unpack Foucault's notion of the gaze that turns in upon the self to survey the self, but parents of impaired children with SEN do not have additional resources to draw upon, based on dealing with day-to-day difficulties and are often reliant on the 'expert gaze'. It is important to remember that parents come into contact with many professionals, all of whom may have different agendas, and different 'expert' stories to tell. It is here the parents continue to get caught up in the private and public realm of SEN. As with '[w]elfare recipients who were expected to have some reciprocal responsibility [to get well, to look after themselves or their families better, to seek work etc.]' (Culpitt, 1999: 145), parents of impaired children feel this to be the case. Parents end up in battles at times with all those they consider to place barriers in the way of their child's education, as they struggle to do what is best for their child, as well coping with the internal battle that goes on as their parenting abilities are doubted.

## Desperation tactics and conflict

After Marlene's oldest child was excluded from school and spent time being educated at home, it seemed clear that she felt far from being in any kind of partnership with the 'experts' and was experiencing great difficulty.

> He's at home and he's suffering because he isn't mixing with anyone. I had a huge to-do over that. We had to lobby like the MP and we was going up to [the LEA] and meeting the head up there ... in the end I took Owen up there and left him. I left him with a pack lunch and said, 'get on with him, you deal with him, there you go. I'm going to bring him everyday here ... and at least he can mix with all your members of staff rather than sit ...' and they said, 'you can't do that' and I said, 'yes I can, watch me'. Prior to that I did phone up social services and tell them what I was going to do, and I still have a social worker [laughs] ... just in case, just in case like they thought they would take him away and they actually said, 'Good on ya ... we're only based on the opposite side of the road so if they do ring us come and collect him from us ... we don't think you're a bad parent we know you're not', because it was social services that also backed us.

Marlene did experience support from social services with regard to what she was doing, and with a struggle she got what she wanted, but this is extreme action and not all parents are able to negotiate these conflicts in this confrontational way.

In an equally confrontational experience (and an extreme desire to gain support), Tracy wanted her youngest to go to a special school, but the mainstream head teacher refused to cooperate in moving this forward. However, after an incident involving the police, Tracy went to the school and told them,

> I'm not taking him home. You do something with him.... . And [the head teacher] finally said, 'look I'm in the middle of penning a letter to the education authority saying that we can't cope', and he said, 'and I'm sorry I was wrong'. I laughed, cried, and smacked him round the

face, all in one go, because it was like after I've gone through another year of hell you've ... but then he wasn't allowed to go back to school anymore and he was at home 24/7 ... for about four months.

The process of educational assessment has meant that most of the parents in this study have been in conflict with either the LEA, social services or other education professionals such as teachers and SENCOs, with problems ranging from lack of support or little communication with the social services, to lack of understanding from teachers and disagreements with the proposals set out by the LEA. Of course not all are in constant battle and some parents have encountered very supportive professionals. Unfortunately they tend to point these out as 'one offs', as Una commented, 'I had this one woman from education and she was brilliant, someone I could really talk to and understand, but she was the only one out of at least 20, if only they were all like her'.

## Conclusions

What promotes the conflict between the parents and the professionals? With the intervention of the state into the private sphere, as discussed by Donzelot (1979), Foucault (1973, 1976) and Wyness (1996), there is an increased notion that the state will therefore provide the tools for the education of all children. However, this is contrasted with the education policies in place to enable parents to have a more involved participatory role in their children's education process. This chapter in many ways is pivotal to the whole process of how parents negotiate, and become *part* of the process of special education and support services. Before this process begins, the parents may either be coming to terms with their baby/child who has been identified as having an impairment, or actually believe they have a baby or child no different from any other, or in fact could be questioning certain behaviours that do not feel 'quite right', as discussed in the previous chapter. While parents may have come into contact with health and social work professionals prior to this assessment process, the education process sees an expansion of professional involvement. It is here there seems to be a point of conflict, if parents and professionals do not see the child's educational future in the same way. However, as I have pointed out, that is not to suggest that professionals are 'baddies' and parents are 'victims'. Both face problems in dealing with these emotional and practical difficulties.

The difficulties go much deeper than the surface struggle between the LEA, class teachers, schools and the parents. In general New Labour and social policy assumes a level of partnership, inclusion and anti-exclusion (see Bowring, 2000; Glendinning et al., 2002; Levitas, 1998; Lister, 1998; Russell, 2003a; Swain and Cook, 2001). The LEAs, teachers and schools are attempting to work within this framework of policy and directives, and the parents are coming to terms with their emotions around having an impaired child. Furthermore, the expectations about each other's role within this process cause conflict between the parties. Therefore, it is not necessarily that the problem lay with the state involvement per se (Foucault, 1973, 1977; Rose, 1989), but that it is more about the parents' dashed expectations of relationships and support structures.

Ian Craib (1994: 3) discusses desire and suggests that it

carries connotations of needing urgently, yearning, to the point almost of trying to will something into existence. Sometimes we desire something so completely that we revert to our infant selves and scream, metaphorically or in reality, in hope that our desire may be realised ...

The parents in this research are struggling with their own desire to have a child without impairment, on top of which have a strong desire to take care of their impaired child, and yet do not seem able to do this without support and help of the special education support services. This official process is not set up for parents, but includes parents. This process also includes the education providers (mainly schools), the LEAs, the health and the social work professionals. The objectives of parents and all others involved should be the same: to meet the needs of the child, and yet bureaucratic measures, finances and levels of need (low to high) dictate how the process, and then provision is delivered. Parents enter this process with certain expectations, often fuelled by emotions alongside a lack of the 'official' knowledge, and therefore partnerships with professionals are difficult.

If parents leave aspects of this work to the special education process then, as with Jack and Kim, the conflict is minimal. Kim took a back seat with her son's education and concentrated on his physiotherapy. Significantly though, she discovered that by the time he reached 15 years his education had not progressed in the way she had expected. She had been to all the annual reviews and the teachers had said, 'he is doing fine'. But they meant fine in relation to their expectations of a child with cerebral palsy, she realised. Not fine for Kim and her son, who were awakened to the fact that he was not going to gain the GCSE results both he and Kim had anticipated. So although Kim's experiences of the school years and reviews were not a traumatic process, her discovery that the statement delivery and SEN process did not work for her son left her feeling that she should have done more and engaged with the process during his school years. Jack found that his youngest son's medical needs were more time consuming with appointments and reviews, and alongside his difficult relationship with their mother, the education aspect of this process took a backseat. Like with any of these situations, education may not always take priority if, for example, medical needs are prioritised.

It is not the fact that many parents do not want the state to play a part in the lives of their impaired child, they often do, but due to discourses within the political sphere they have expectations that professionals will listen and take on board what they have to say about their child's difficulties and outside a financial set of goals. Most expect professionals to be available as a support system for themselves and their children, rather than a group of 'experts' to fear or fight. For instance, Debbie and Tracy wanted some kind of help, child or family therapy, but support was not forthcoming. Beresford (1995: 10) also found this and notes that one parent said, 'I'd like family therapy to help us all cope and learn how best to deal with this and express it'. Unfortunately, as with Lynne and Francis, the emphasis was not on support but on apportioning blame.

This chapter has been about unpacking parental narratives within an SEN policy and professional framework. It richly described how parents experience and negotiate this SEN process, and in turn how it affects them emotionally, practically and financially. The following chapter explores how parents experience the actual education provision alongside expectations and disappointments regarding 'inclusion' within mainstream schools.

# 5
# Experiencing a 'Special' Education

> Educational success becomes a function of social, cultural and material advantages in which mothers' caring within the family is transmuted by the operations of the wider marketplace to serve its competitive, self-interested, individualistic ethos. Mothers' practical maintenance, educational and emotional work underpins the workings of educational markets, contributing to a culture of winners and losers within which one child's academic success is at the expense of other children's failure.
>
> (Reay, 1998: 165)

Parents in Britain, and indeed much of the Western world, can assume their child will be educated, and that the education provided will probably be carried out within a school. It is part of the socialisation process. For parents in this study, education provision is not a straightforward process whereby the child goes to school, engages with a curriculum and learns how to develop intellectually and conform to and manage social norms. Parents in this study have children who do not merge easily into this social world.

This chapter is divided into five sections. The first is about parents' hopes and desires for mainstream education for their child and what they expect of the school and the staff involved in their child's education. The second follows the same theme, but instead of concentrating on the desire for the mainstream school, it focuses on adverse reactions to the special school, abnormality and aversion to difficult difference. The third, documents parental stories of the special school both with positive and negative experiences. The fourth section focusses on exclusion and the 'difficult' and disruptive child, and the fifth deals with experiences of residential education provision. The main aim of this chapter is to document and analyse how mothers and fathers negotiate the education process and highlight how difficult this process can be.

All of the children in this research entered the English school system between the late 1980s and 2002. Between them, the 24 parents had 30 children identified with SEN. At the time of the interview, 12 of these children had spent all their school years, in mainstream education, albeit some with one-to-one support. Significantly, the youngest group (up to eight years old) comprised the largest group in mainstream school. There were no youths aged 15 years and above who had spent their entire school years in mainstream education. These figures are significant because education policy and directives in England and Wales suggest mainstream school for all children (where possible), and yet by the time these children reach transitional ages – 7, 11, 16 and 18, as my research suggests – mainstream education can, in certain circumstances, become increasingly difficult. In this chapter I illustrate this with stories of special education, mainstream education and alternatives, and show how parents experience different education placements. Many of the parents in this research have experienced more than one type of special education and, like with the rest of the experiences in the book, it is often not a linear process.

## Parental hopes for mainstream education

All 24 of the parents in this research initially expected that their child would be educated in a mainstream environment regardless of their child's impairment, especially those entering the school system after 1997 under New Labour. As highlighted in Chapter 1, policy and directives suggest all children are considered for mainstream school in the first instance. Different groups of children with varying degrees of abilities all in the same place follow a similar, if not the same, curriculum. However, at a theoretical level this desire to make everyone 'fit' within a certain mould creates an illusion of an unfragmented, homogenous group. In practice this cannot happen within the current mainstream school system; moreover, is it desirable?

Ian Craib (1994: 104) suggests that in Western society, '[t]he existence of large scale bureaucratic organisations creates expectations of orderliness and predictability, so we come to expect the same from ourselves' our own family education and emotional life. The official education process that underpins and attempts to govern how parents engage with such a structure is set up, at best, to disappoint, if parents and the education professionals consider mainstream (inclusive) education to be the best option for the impaired child. This ideal of an inclusive education system theoretically runs parallel with the idea that family life should be uncomplicated and stable to a certain extent, as with expectations of mothering and childrearing. 'This is a dream of emotional management, in the sense of expecting a stable and ordered emotional life, and if that does not occur, the assumption is that something is wrong' (Craib 1994: 104). This section describes parents' hopes and highlights the disappointment in realising mainstream education is an unrealistic option.

### Mainstream: an expectation

Tim wanted his son, who has Down's syndrome, to go to the local mainstream school. However, after that proved difficult in practice, because the mainstream school was unable to support his son's needs, he assumed the next best thing would be the local school for children with MLD. Significantly, the MLD school was unable to manage his son's impairments, so he was then transferred to a local school for children with severe learning difficulties (SLD). Tim first told me about mainstream primary school.

> I think if you take stage one at [the local mainstream], I think stage one was an optimistic go for things ... on that one, to be honest we hadn't overly invested ... it was nice to have a go at it and if it had worked out that would have been great ... that was always a long shot and therefore when that didn't materialise that didn't really worry us.... But we really felt that the headmaster ... and to be blunt what you could have said, let's face it you just couldn't fucking well be bothered, but you're not allowed to say that ... I mean in that respect we was pissed off, but that's only small beer really to be pissed of like that ... it's no big shock to us because we thought it was a long shot anyway.

Significantly, even though Tim would have liked his son to go to the mainstream school, and indeed expected his schooling to begin there, it was not a complete shock that the placement failed. His son's second placement in the MLD school was a different matter; as Tim explained, his son became unhappy there.

> The [MLD] school came as more of a ... kind of surprise ... I think in some ways we were a bit more distant really because he was then picked up ... no [my wife] used to drop him off in the car ... it was

a gradual feeling that he didn't seem terribly keen to go to school and he seemed unhappy. They didn't choose to say what had gone wrong at that school but that Barry's not the first and won't be the last to move from there.

Tim was disappointed that the MLD placement did not work out, but in fact his son was better placed in the SLD school. Because Tim said that his son was happier there, being one of the high achievers within a group of children that had severe learning impairments.

Karen too wanted mainstream education for her son with Down's syndrome, and said, 'of the nine years of fighting I managed to get half a day for him at [mainstream primary school]. His own school just round the corner would not take him despite what it said in the statement' (*the statement of SEN had named the local mainstream primary as the school for Kevin*). The rest of Karen's son's education, thus far, has been carried out in a school for children with MLD. But she has continued to appeal against decisions made because of the difficulties her son had in coping with the first MLD placement.

Una, who had spent time as a helpline manager for a charity which supports parents of children with impairments, described her thoughts in both her professional capacity and as a parent with her own hopes for mainstream education.

When parents come onto the help line particularly when the kids are very young there is a complete and total expectation that their child will attend the local mainstream school. And I was one of those parents too. It's only when you go through watching your child damaged that you are likely to change your mind about that.

It is quite clear from these cases that the parents do have an expectation for their child to attend mainstream school. However, as suggested above, the *expectations* of their child being included and accepted into the mainstream school environment may not be in fact the reality of an inclusive education system, as it currently exists.

My research suggests that parents and their impaired children have difficulty with the mainstream environment, but other research also confirms that mainstream education can be problematic: see Allan (1999), Benjamin (2002), Norwich (2000) and Wilson (1999). However, conversely, if Richard Rieser, a prominent member of the National Union of Teachers (NUT) and head of the Disability and Equality in Education pressure group, was to have his way, all special schools would be closed by 2020, otherwise 'there could be future generations of kids who will continue to have their lives ruined' (Hilpern, 2004). This study suggests otherwise, as illustrated by Tracy and her mainstream experience.

## Dealing with difficulty: a mainstream experience

Tracy has four sons; two of them have been identified with different impairments. The oldest is a twin, David, identified with hydrocephalus (water on the brain) and mild cerebral palsy as well as moderate learning impairments. He spent his primary school years in mainstream education, and at 11, he moved to a school for children with MLD. He then went on to mainstream college at 16. Tracy's youngest son, Brad, however, spent his primary years at mainstream schools, but at the age of nine was excluded and received home tuition for four months due to his disruptive anti-social behaviour. He was then transferred to a residential school for children with EBD.

In talking about her oldest child, Tracy revealed it was a miracle that David survived after the birth. Looking back, she said, thinking about his education was not on her list of priorities. His health and life expectancy were more important. However, by the time it came to sending her twins to school she did expect they would go to the same local mainstream primary school. David wore a shunt in his skull to drain the fluid from his brain, and had a limp from the mild cerebral palsy, but to Tracy was 'a delightful lad'. Bearing in mind special education policy specifies that all children, where possible, should be included within mainstream school, it is not surprising that parents expect their children to at least begin their school career in mainstream education.

Significantly, three of the children mentioned above had an 'obvious' impairment, two with Down's syndrome and the other (Tracy's son) with hydrocephalus and cerebral palsy. Not only can the educational professionals *see* the impairment, and have an assumption about what that impairment means, but the parent also expects the child will have some difficulties, unlike parents who have a child identified with, for example, AS or AD/HD, when the identification may come later on in their school career and the impairment is less visible. Nevertheless, Tracy did expect David to attend the local mainstream school with his twin brother. Prior to Tracy sending David to the local mainstream primary she had long conversations with one of the LEA officers about his impairments. She also visited the school where he had been accepted, but had not met with the head teacher. She was told David could attend that school, but what was to follow on the first day highlights the sort of shameless prejudice parents can encounter.

It was hard enough for Tracy to let her twin boys go off to school for their first day, as it is for many mothers, but it was doubly difficult to 'let go' of David, whom she had already spent so much of her time 'nursing', in addition to mothering, in the hope that she would one day be seeing him off to school. This was the reception she received when she went to pick them up at the end of their first day.

> I came back to pick them up at the end of the day and erm ... as I walked into the playground the teacher went [beckoned] like to me and the headmistress went [beckoned] and I went over to them and she said, 'into my office please'. I thought they can't have been naughty like that on the first day! She got me in her office. She said, 'take a seat. I wasn't aware I was having a bloody retard in my school' [she's curt], ... I went mental, absolutely mental ... I threw her round the room. I did totally freak out.

Tracy continued to explain her actions:

> Well there's a lot ... they go to school for the first time anyway, you're a bit lost, especially with your first children, child whatever ... I built up their enthusiasm about going and I'm as excited for them and I'd missed, erm, and to be going into school to collect them expecting to go in and say hello darlings did you have a good day and I got that! Plus I was on my own with them by that time.

The police were called in and Tracy was arrested and when she told the police what had happened, 'they said, "well I'd have hit her as well"'. She was cautioned and sent home, but later on an education officer visited her and she was given a full written and verbal apology. Furthermore, the head teacher was advised to drop the charges or face disciplinary action. Tracy did not go back to that school and moved geographically. Tracy's twin sons were absent from school for five weeks but then settled into a new mainstream primary, until secondary transition at 11 years old.

Unlike Karen, who has fought for years to try to get her son into mainstream school, and Tim, who eventually accepted that his son would go to an SEN school, as did Una, Tracy began to push for a special school placement after realising that her son was not getting the education she thought he needed in the mainstream primary school. Even though she was worried that he might emulate 'anti-social' or inappropriate behaviour if he attended a special school, she decided to appeal to the LEA for a SEN placement.

The following example was one of the reasons for her deciding upon this action after attending a parents' evening and chatting to his teacher.

> There was a comment one of the teachers made, 'oh David's a lovely boy, we all adore him, he's so sweet'.... And she said, 'David found the maths lesson a bit difficult so I sent him outside to cut the heads of the daffodils, the dead heads'. And that was David's math lesson. That really annoyed me ... that's when I started pushing for him to go to a special school.

There are a few things going on here, not least the fact that often a child who has learning difficulties but no significant EBD and remains in mainstream school can often be looked upon as 'lovable', 'cute' or 'sweet' inferring that he or she is different and even uneducable in the same way as his or her peers, but very much liked as a member of the class, bearing in mind this child does *not* disrupt the class. But to be liked is not enough when it comes to the question of the child's education and esteem.

My daughter, in fact, was a quiet and very personable girl. She would often be described, as 'sweet' and 'cute' and people would say, 'you're so lucky she's well behaved', but this is not always helpful. Una described her son's experience in similar terms.

> He was not unhappy but he became the school mascot ... he was a loveable young man, erm ... but the difference between their ability to give him an education that has any meaning, and what he has received since then [in residential SEN schools] could not be more chalk and cheese.

Allan (1999: 32) talks of deserving and undeserving education, as she describes how pupils view their peers with SEN. This, as I have said, is certainly evident with the children in this study who do not have additional EBD.

> The peers of Brian, a 12-year-old with Down's syndrome, talked about him with warmth and affection and frequent laughter because they 'loved being with him' and 'he was such a lot of fun', despite being 'a bit of a handful'. He had not been 'as lucky as them, when he was born, but they are humans, so should be treated the same as us'.

However, not all children experience the same 'warmth'. Allan (1999: 33) also found that children with SEN who do not have 'obvious' impairments are often viewed as problematic within a mainstream environment as described here:

> The classmates of Peter, a 12-year-old identified as having emotional or behavioural difficulties, were highly uncertain about where to place him on the deserving/undeserving divide. This arose from their difficulty in understanding what was actually 'wrong with him'. Without the high visibility of a medical condition or some other clue to a disability, it was difficult for Peter's peers to make sense of his simultaneously odd and normal behaviour.

These two patterns clearly link back to Tracy's experience of mainstream school and her two impaired children. David, a twin with obvious impairments but no behavioural problems, did in fact, contrary to Tracy's wishes, remain in mainstream primary school until secondary transition and subsequently went to an SEN secondary school at the age of 11. Brad, whose syndrome presented with behavioural problems, had difficulties in mainstream education from a young age, and was excluded by the time he was nine years old.

What much of the research in this area indicates is that although parents and policy directives may initially promote mainstream education for impaired children, the older the child is, the less likely mainstream practices work, based on both the inherent difficulties of teaching large classes, differentiating work and dealing with difficulty. However, parents' *expectation* of mainstream education is not simply about policy and directives, but also about a deeper cultural aversion to difference, difficulty and intellectual impairment as described in the following section.

## Adverse reactions to the 'special' school

It is clear that Tracy and the other parents in this research wanted mainstream provision initially, but is this simply about choosing to include a child within mainstream based on expectations for the child and policy directives? Or is this about *not* wanting the alternative, based on preconceived perceptions about the special school? Many of the parents in this research have grown up with assumptions about children in special schools being a type of underclass, almost below humanity. In this section I unpack some of their initial attitudes towards special schools, and engage with literature that parallels some of these prejudices and fears. Some of the parents were very explicit about the reasons why they did not want their child to go to a special school. In the main, this is about perceptions of the special schools and the children who go there for two reasons: either not wanting their child to integrate with children who they feel are more 'abnormal' and more 'different', or not wanting the child to be excluded from mainstream society and the 'real' world. With regard to (dis)association, at the point of coming to terms with their child's impairment, the parents may then have to associate their child with others who have more visible or different impairments. (Think about the link here in chapter three with reference to denial or disassociation with a more severe impairment). This is especially true of those parents who consider their child to have 'non visible difficulties' like speech and language disorders, and more importantly do not want to consider their child as being *learning* impaired.

## Facing the uncomfortable

Kerry was satisfied that both her sons were receiving appropriate education in specialist residential placements when I last interviewed her in 2002. However, that was not the case in the first instance. Gary, the oldest, was transferred from mainstream primary and the youngest, Ian was transferred from a school for children with MLD to a residential special school. Initially Kerry did not want an SEN placement for either of her children. With Gary, she told me, 'I knew I didn't want him to go to a special school because I know that it was *only* speech and language'. Until the age of seven, Gary was happy in mainstream, and Kerry says that the head teacher was 'excellent'. However, she told me, 'I feel this vibe that they are hinting that Gary may have to go ... go to a special school....' Kerry was adamant too that Ian, her second son, would also go to mainstream school, but the teachers at Gary's mainstream school were already beginning to struggle with his social and educational needs, which had a direct influence on teachers and the LEA placing Ian, and therefore did not suggest mainstream provision for him.

When Kerry was told by the LEA and the school that Ian should go to a school for children with MLD, she stressed she was 'gutted, absolutely gutted', but she visited it all the same. Her reaction was one of horror and highlighted this fact not only in the first interview, but also in the second as well, in relation to placing Gary.

I was absolutely horrified when I went. There were children with severe learning disabilities and severely handicapped ... children rolling round, there were children spitting, making noises ... dribbling, some weren't even able to hold themselves up. ... There were quite a few children who looked abnormal, Down's ... there were a few with Down's ... there were some that looked perfectly normal but when they spoke!

Kerry's husband, from whom she separated during this research, also went to the school and she told me his reaction was very different. He was quite positive and she retold what he said, 'it doesn't matter what children are like there as long as Gary gets the attention and the teaching skills to help him'. Kerry at that point did not feel like that, and simply could not see past her own initial prejudices about the special school and the denial of her sons having any intellectual impairments.

Tracy was less explicit regarding her concerns about David going to a special school, but still revealed,

> what I was worried about with David, was that he was a copier, he would copy other people ... I was worried that he'd go to a special school where they were all a lot worse than him and rather than learn anything he'd sit there rocking, dribbling and banging his head on the wall.

These attitudes to that of dribbling, head banging and grunting clearly tap into perceptions about socially acceptable behaviour as well as deeper perceptions informed by fear of the unknown. There seem to be concerns about the 'special' school from the mothers here at different levels. For some there are assumptions made about the visible grossness of the other children's behaviour. They perceive their child to be outside a particular impaired group. Fear, which then comes with their child being associated with that group, is compounded by the possibility of their child copying the 'anti-social' behaviour, and so becoming like the 'disabled other'.

### Who's the enemy?

With regard to fear, Susan Sontag's (1991) philosophical essays *Illness as Metaphor and AIDS and its Metaphors* are revealing when paralleled with disability and impairment. She unpacks the myths and metaphors mainly around tuberculosis and cancer in the first essay, and then in the second, AIDS with syphilis and leprosy. Fear of the unknown and, more importantly, the fear of not wanting association with anti-social behaviour and visible impairment can frighten parents because they have their own assumptions about wholesome aesthetics and what it means to be human. 'The most terrifying illnesses are those perceived not just as lethal but as dehumanising, literally so' (Sontag 1991: 124), like leprosy, or in this case, an impairment; '[t]he most dreaded are those that seem like mutations into animality' (ibid.: 126–7). Shakespeare (1994: 296) too writes about this repulsion of animality or impairment and notes that

> [t]he peculiar and particular fascination – the fear and loathing – that disability has for human beings is because impairment represents the physicality and animality of human existence. Nature is the enemy, women are the enemy, black people are the enemy, disabled people are the enemy.

Sibley (1995: 51), the geographer, reiterates this by suggesting, 'those threatening people beyond the boundary represent the features of human existence from which the civilized have distanced themselves – close contact with nature, dirt, excrement, overt sexuality ...' (all of which have been associated with some of my participants' children). It may be considered that 'normality' goes beyond a project of 'normalisation' and to a place in the psyche where fear and disgust lie dormant. Similarly, it can be argued aberration of the 'untamed' (Swift, 1967 [1726]), the 'impure' (Douglas, 1966), the 'dangerous' (Young, 1999) and 'imperfect' (Chadwick, 1987) are currently glossed over in current public discourse as highlighted in the rhetoric of inclusive education.

### The 'real' mainstream world?

Not wanting a special school, for some parents, is not explicitly about a disassociation from, or aversion to, others with impairments, but more of a concern about wanting their child to mix with 'normal' peers, with a view to emulating socially acceptable behaviour. The second theme in this section was that of the parents' concerns about the child being isolated from his or her mainstream peers. Neil's son, identified with ASD, in response to the suggestion of attendance at a language unit, said,

> It's one of those things like when you're told your child's got a language problem you do just think language problem child, language unit, 2 + 2 = 4. But it's not as simple as that. I'm concerned with the fact that if he's in a language unit he'd be ghettoised. He does ever so well with his normal peers ... normal ... whatever you call it and I don't want him to be ghettoised. I know they say in the language unit they integrate in the normal school, that they're part of it ... but as a teacher I know what integration means and it isn't always as easy ... it's not as easy as they'd like it to be.

Neil continued with the process of assessment for the language unit even though he and his wife wanted a mainstream placement. The assumption was that if his son was not accepted due to lack of places, he would be able to defend a mainstream placement in response to the LEA, and said, 'we feel that we can use that as ammunition for getting him speech therapy'. In a way, what Neil explained is not so different to the reactions of the mothers above, only he emphasises the positive aspects and the more policy-driven notion of the mainstream environment, i.e., mixing with his 'normal' peers, and not wanting his son to be ghettoised in a special school. Neil here is implicit rather than explicit in his aversion to the SEN school. Nonetheless, the implication is the same for the child with regard to negative assumptions about 'special' schools and the desire to be in a school with 'normal' children.

Kim, whose son was born with mild cerebral palsy, did not want him to go to a special school. Like Neil, her aversion to SEN schools was implicit.

> I really found it a hard decision to make and I came to the conclusion that it might be better to put him into what I say is the 'real world' and have to face people that say things about him, and it might be a battle for him but if he's capable of it isn't it better that he goes into see what the real world's about...? I was with a slightly disabled child. ... Mainstream seemed too harsh and you know ... special school I thought may hold him back because he was capable of more.

Kim explicitly and on more than one occasion talks of the harsh 'real' world and the 'cotton wool like, SEN world'. Kim's son spent all of his school life (until 16 years old) in mainstream school and she separated her view of worlds, and discussed openly with her son that there was this harsher 'real' world. Kim's son's positive experience as a teenager attending a sports club for physically impaired students and his negative experience at the mainstream comprehensive led him to a post-16 college for students with impairments. With Kim's help he decided upon a residential one, where according to her he has flourished and grown in confidence.

For many of the parents in this study, their struggle was with the desire for their child to be 'normal'. This desire leads the parent to either disassociate their child from other children who have more severe impairments, and deny their child has a significant impairment, or attempt to integrate their impaired child into mainstream school with a view that mainstream schools constitute part of the 'real' world. Significantly, many parents associate impairment and disability with the loss of a limb, or hearing and sight, but their children's impairments can be equally disabling and in need of specialist support with their lack of communication and/or spatial awareness, coordination and/or comprehension difficulties. It is understandable, therefore, that the parents are confused about the 'disabled' status of their impaired child, causing conflict with assumptions about provision within a 'special' school or not.

## Experiences within the 'special' school

Almost half of the children in this study have experienced some kind of specialist teaching in a separate unit or education site (not including those who went straight from mainstream to residential school). Out of these, 11 have attended a special school for either moderate or severe learning disabilities. Two have attended language units and one a pupil referral unit (PRU). We have already heard that, for some mothers, the thought of a special school was initially horrific: Kerry, Karen and Stella initially did not want special schools for their sons. Yet Kerry and Stella found this to be the more appropriate placement, and their children flourished. Jack, whose sons attended a school for children with MLD, and Tim, who we have already heard about, were more accepting of the special school placement, even in the first instance.

Karen and Stella have had two different experiences regarding special education for their sons. Both are divorced and single parents. Stella considered herself lucky at 'discovering' Nathan's school for children with MLD. Nathan was born with a 'brain disorder' and a possible diagnosis of ASD. Karen, on the other hand, found the whole experience (including special education) frustrating and continued to want mainstream education for Kevin, born with Down's syndrome, who also attends a school for children with MLD.

### Positive support: the early years

Karen's son Kevin has attended two different MLD schools, but at the age of nine Karen managed (after a struggle) to get him into a mainstream school for half a day, 'and then after much jumping up and down was extended to one day, but I was never allowed to have more than one day ... that was the only time in mainstream'. Kevin was statemented during his first year at primary school although the process began at nursery. He had what Karen called a 0–5 teacher from the LEA who went to her house to teach him. 'She was a trained teacher and very very good, you know she'd come for an hour and give you ideas about what she'd want you to do, erm ... she was very very keen for Kevin to go to mainstream and I wanted him to go to mainstream'. Stella too had this very positive experience from the 0–5 services and told me,

> I had Maggie who was working for the 0–5 service. And she was fantastic 'cause when she came in ... she just came in and supported Nathan in the home and she taught me so much ... I've learnt ... she empowered me! That's the word isn't it? No she did, she was fantastic.

Both these examples clearly indicate that the pre-school services were well supported and received by both Karen and Stella, and yet neither experienced this level of positive support after school began.

### Juggling excessive difficulties: home and school

The local mainstream school that Karen told me was named on Kevin's statement had a change of head teacher. Karen explained that the new head teacher 'decided' that she did not want a child with Down's syndrome in her school: (recall Tracy's experience with the head teacher above). Karen wanted Kevin to go to mainstream school, but at that point had not met the new head teacher and so he automatically went to the local MLD school. (This goes against the policies on all children attending mainstream school in the first instance). Karen explained to me that she used to try to speak to the head teacher of the local primary school; Karen reiterated the head teacher's response,

> '*speak to county, speak to county!*' [Karen screeched this]. She would never speak to me. She took one look at his statement and her face fell. Because presumably she saw that her school was named in the statement. She would never speak to me again. She NEVER met Kevin; she never spoke to Kevin.

Kevin never went to that school and Karen did not fight at that point, partly because she had to deal with the day-to-day difficulties with her son and his deteriorating behaviour at the MLD school he was attending. She spent much of her time trying to get him *out* of that school rather than into mainstream per se.

Karen clearly had some difficulties with talking about her experiences with his first MLD placement and told me, 'it's the most dreadful school you can ever imagine in your life ...' [Her voice faltered here]. She went on and told me there had been allegations of sexual and physical abuse. (Tracy too discussed issues about physical abuse, and the residential school her youngest son attended. The police were involved and her son had been one of the boys to be allegedly abused. The school shut down for a short period of time but her son never went back there. Since then her son was a legal witness in a legal case indicating the vulnerability of these children.) These are additional and excessive difficulties for parents of children with impairments as they are well aware of the vulnerability of their children. Karen was not saying that her son had been sexually abused, but she said that he was clearly disturbed and intimated at allegations as expressed here:

> My son shut down completely and I had to go and pick him up a couple of times because the school had phoned me up, he was actually semi-comatose, I had to carry him out. ... The teacher never appeared; she never spoke to me. I never met her actually. She never came to me.

It is hardly surprising that Karen did not want her son to continue in special education given these experiences of the first school Kevin attended. But for Karen her difficulties with the first special school mapped onto all special schools, however, as we see with Stella below, and other parents in this research, specialist education, for most, has been a positive option. It is clear though, that living with impairment is not simply about 'choice' of school, but an accumulation of all day-to-day experiences, as illustrated in the following chapter.

Karen's relationships with the first MLD school professionals seemed problematic in the first instance, and diminished even further when her third son was born. She communicated less with the school because she was too busy with a young baby. In addition to this Kevin was sick most Sunday nights or Monday mornings. As I understand, it is clear that Kevin was trying to communicate to Karen that he really did not want to go to the school, and on reflection Karen too realised that this was his only way of communicating he did not want to go to school. But admitted that she was unable to read those signs at the time. Eventually though, things became so desperate that Kevin used to 'smack his own bottom and send himself to the corner, he used to get very very cross with his toys', and Karen recalled that her son would shout,

> 'TALK, TALK, TALK' [she said this very aggressively] ... because he'd stopped talking at school ... he'd stopped cooperating ... and his mind ... if you sat quietly in the corner, you know other people

would ignore you, and you wouldn't get what was coming to you ... there was one teacher and class room assistant that he was particularly frightened of.

Because of her son's deteriorating behaviour at the school and home, the LEA's EP had explicitly told Karen that her son would not be able to go to mainstream school even though Karen was still pursuing this.

In Kevin's second year at the MLD primary school she withdrew him and kept him at home as she had serious concerns about his mental and physical health. But she also had to consider her own mental health.

> What happens to your child is they become so awful that they're difficult ... they're too difficult to cope with. And erm ... I insisted that ... one day Kevin was so dreadful ... and I phone up social services and said, 'you'll have to take him away now, this minute because I'm going to kill him'. I said, 'I can't keep all three in separate rooms', he kept clawing at [her older son's] face, he kept attacking the baby and erm ... so they came and got him, and when I went back for him the next day she said, 'Karen, Kevin is not well! He's ill', 'I know he's ill but nobody wants to know'.

What this clearly suggests is that Karen needed respite from the difficulty of dealing with her family, and more specifically her impaired son's behaviour, but Karen's difficulty was not helped by her concerns for her son and a school she considered inappropriate, so much so, that she withdrew him.

Karen found an alternative MLD school some 15 miles away, attended a meeting with the head teacher there, and Kevin was accepted. Kevin continued his school career there and although his behaviour improved Karen still had to collect her son from the school when he had an 'outburst'. Karen finds the lack of communication between her and the teachers difficult. For Karen discussions about whether 'inclusion' is appropriate and necessary seem low down on the agenda as she has a hard enough time dealing with her son practically and emotionally on a day-to-day basis. For example, she explained,

> I had a phone call from [the head teacher] and this bellowing in the background 'I'm sorry Karen can you come up to the school?' and I said, 'no problem. I'll come'. And Kevin's sitting there still moaning and groaning and getting himself in a state and there's this classroom assistant all het up and [the head teacher] is all het up and Kevin had bitten [the head teacher] so had his choppers on him and he's all

upset and couldn't calm him down and I ... he said 'I think you'll have to take him home now and we'll talk later on the phone'.

Problems going on here for Karen are about the official process of negotiating the 'special' education system and the emotional trauma of dealing with difficulty, such as being a lone parent to three children, having a child with impairments, having a bad experience with education professionals and having alleged abuse at the back of her mind. All this took its toll on her. If nothing else, it is manifestly obvious that Karen, and others like her, need support and respite, not only in times of crisis, but regularly, to live with the difficulties incurred, rather than simply coping on a day-to-day basis.

### So your child's different? Positively special

Stella, on the other hand, had extremely positive experiences at her son's special school. As mentioned earlier, Stella wanted mainstream education for Nathan but did go and view two special schools. Stella's experience of Nathan's MLD school has been very positive.

> I was saying to my sister, 'I don't think Nathan's achieving anything in [mainstream] school' and I realised that I had to consider other options and when I look back ... which is why I'm so passionate about it now ... is the fact it [special education] wasn't seen to be a positive option. So I'm ... I want to say to parents with children who are three and four and five, special needs schools are a positive option.

For Stella this process of going into special education has been a journey of discovering that her child *is* different from other children who attend mainstream school, and that it is not a negative or defeatist experience to accept that difference.

> I think it was so hard to be a parent of a child with special needs ... because you don't really know what to expect, you don't really know what to look for ... and it's emotionally traumatic ... you've got to think your child's different ... I think that parents ... if their child's in mainstream school their child's less different.

What Stella implied here, and later discussed, were issues about inclusion and explained,

> I think you'd find most parents if you were talking to them would say in an ideal world inclusion sounds jolly right, super and that's

what I wanted for Nathan, but then you have to think about realism and if you go into a mainstream school and you've got class of 30 able children ... my other son is quite able but you know he'd get much more attention if he was in a class of 15 and he'd achieve more.

As with Stella, some of the other parents whose children have experienced special schools agree that although they initially wanted mainstream education for their children, since experiencing their child's impairments and the mainstream environment, they have had to reconsider their views on what the current government promotes as inclusive education.

I mean they were talking about closing down all the special schools and integrating all the special needs children into mainstream ... I think that would be a disaster. I think there's very much a place for special schools.

(Tracy)

They talk about access, they talk about inclusion, and if your disability is visible then you're ok ... if it can't be easily seen or easily understood you're a bit scary.

(Babs)

I don't agree with it [inclusion] at all for children with speech and language problems, particularly with receptive disorders because ...they barely understand what the teacher is saying.

(Tina)

These parents are concerned that inclusive education does not work, based on their everyday experiences, and that their children have benefited from a different type of education.

Similarly, in Russell's (2003b: 148) research on 'disability and parental expectations' one mother said, 'I think I had quite a simplistic idea that because policy in this authority seems to be so much towards integration then the schools would reflect that but I didn't find that they did'. And she went on to say: 'I think they [the teachers] see it as an extra burden to have a statemented child in their class. So how it actually works in practice really concerns me' (ibid.).

Karen and Stella's experiences were very different, but those differences illustrate a number of things. Not only is it the child's impairment that can make the difference with regard to different experiences. But parents' expectations, hopes, desires, wishes *and* emotional responses that parents take into the relationships with professionals and others are crucial in the way difference is experienced. Their cultural expectations and personal circumstances can have a huge impact. These predictions, and indeed life courses, are very difficult to cater for within the political sphere, but need to be considered all the same. However, practical difficulties and emotional responses *are* messy and unpredictable.

So far in this chapter I have uncovered what parents' expectations are, and their responses to a special education. The following section reveals that mainstream education may not be the most appropriate, especially if the impaired child does not have significant intellectual impairments, but has EBD.

## Experiencing exclusion: the child *and* the parent

This section demonstrates, mainly via Marlene's story, the problem of exclusion and the mainstream school, both in relation to the child's exclusion from mainstream education and the mother's exclusion and isolation. Inclusive education policy and directives, for example DfES (2001a, 2001b) and literature which celebrates 'difference' (Young, 1999), seem abstract for many of the parents, as they and their child may not experience anything like an integrated inclusive education or indeed social inclusion and acceptance.

Inclusion into mainstream school is not simply about the placement of a child. The child with impairments that present in some kind of anti-social behaviour seems to have a significant chance of exclusion from and within mainstream school. The child that does not disrupt the teaching regime and sits quietly (as in the case of Una, Tracy's oldest, and my own daughter) is often not excluded from the mainstream environment as quickly (if at all) as a child who cannot explicitly cope with noise, certain lighting, other children or instructions, for example.

Benjamin, in her ethnographic research on the 'micropolitics of inclusive education', found that children with impairments that present with behavioural difficulties, for example, ASD, can cause conflict for their teachers and the other students within the mainstream school environment, as illustrated here. Josie, a student identified with autism, was in her first year at secondary school and clearly struggling.

> Her continued placement was always in doubt: officially because she had not made sufficient progress in terms of her IEP [individual education plan], and unofficially because she was ungovernable and because people's good will towards someone who enacted her difference in

demanding ways had been exhausted. Two days before her review was scheduled, she was part of a 'serious incident'. She had been in a fight with another girl who then involved some friends, one who made fun of Josie. Josie panicked, and began to hit and kick the girl, shouting that she would kill her ... [Josie] was detained by three male teachers. The teachers took her into the school office [the nearest room available] where she caused considerable damage to property before the three men and myself as a witness could corral her behind a desk. Eventually Josie's uncle arrived to take her home. She was not allowed back on the premises. At her annual review, Josie's placement was formally terminated, and a placement in segregated special provision recommended.

(Benjamin, 2002: 126–7)

This excerpt from Benjamin's research is not dissimilar to some of the stories told to me by parents, as highlighted below. Not unsurprisingly, some of the parents in my study either feel ambivalent towards the inclusionary policies or vehemently disagree that inclusive education can work.

Una, as we have heard, wanted mainstream education for her son, but realising the damage it was doing stated quite categorically:

What I'm increasingly seeing now ... and local authorities are going gung ho for, inclusion at secondary level. The children get dumped in bottom classes even when they're quite bright because nobody actually understands how to teach them and where that isn't the case what they end up with is a scenario where there are all these children being taught by learning support assistants. Well I don't know about anybody else, but I think as a parent, I think my child has a right to be taught by teachers who are qualified. But I think then there's the question that needs to be asked: how much can you ask a mainstream class teacher to do in terms of teaching a range of difficulties, and what are we actually asking the education authority to do here in promoting inclusion? Now many of the actual physical school sites are too big, the children can't cope with the class sizes, with the noise levels and you know, the bounciness of it all, which is fine, great at one level but at another level it's very damaging for a lot of our children.

Una in her line of work has also heard many other parents' stories via the helpline with regard to negative stories in relation to 'inclusion' and mainstream schools.

From the stories in this research, it seems there are many children who are included in the mainstream education but are excluded at different levels.

- *Practically* – they are often removed from the class for one-to-one work in an individual teaching unit.
- *Intellectually* – they often cannot access the curriculum in the same way their peers do.
- *Emotionally* – their difficulties can preclude them from sustaining friendship networks and engaging with others socially.

The following illuminate these aspects of exclusions.

### Marlene: Owen's exclusions

Marlene, a working-class mother, has three sons, all of whom have been identified with impairments. The youngest is visually impaired and has moderate learning impairments; the middle son has been identified with AS, SPLD and OCD. Owen, whom I shall be discussing in more detail, has been identified with both AS and AD/HD. The two younger ones are currently in a mainstream primary school. Owen on the other hand, five years older than his youngest brother, has been excluded from two mainstream primary schools and spent three terms in a PRU. At the time of our second interview, Marlene was looking for a mainstream secondary school that would 'include' him. Marlene wanted a small school with small classes, because, like Josie in Benjamin's (2002) research, he was unable to cope with large groups of people.

Owen, at the age of six and seven, would constantly run away from school if not supervised. Throughout Owen's primary years teachers told Marlene that he was simply a badly behaved child. During this time she actually said to the teachers 'you have to hold on to him. You have to make sure you see me. It's no good him saying he's seen me 'cause quite often he'd say he can see me and I wasn't there'. Marlene constantly received phone calls from the school saying that Owen had run away, or 'can you pick him up as he's rolling around on the headmistress's floor'. By the time Owen was seven he had seen an EP and had been referred to a PRU. The main objective of such placements is to attempt to control a child's behaviour and return them to mainstream. Owen was in a PRU for three terms, and during that time, Marlene explained,

> his self esteem come up you know ... his behaviour improved, his work come on in leaps and bounds erm ... but unfortunately the

maximum they keep them there was the three terms. It seems to be a short sharp shock, get them in and get them out ... but if you've got problems like my Owen got you can't get them in get them out and turn them around, because what he's got it's life long ... but up until then he'd only been diagnosed with the AD/HD. I think it was still seen as just a behaviour problem. 'We'll get him in there, turn him around and put him back into mainstream and he'll be fine'. He went back into mainstream and he wasn't fine. They put him in a different school. The headmistress said that basically she didn't want him back.

Exclusion for Owen, as with some of the other children, is not experienced on one level as indicated above. He was still on the school roll (register) while attending the PRU, but the head teacher 'asked him' not to sit for the statutory assessment tests (SATs) because, as Marlene believed, 'she didn't want his results bringing her league table down. And the LEA agreed to it, that was fine'. Then the head teacher excluded Owen by not wanting him back.

Owen was not the only one excluded or withdrawn from SATs in this research, as Debbie found when she wanted to take her son away to reduce the pressure on him. 'The school and LEA were happy for me to take him away. The school gave us their blessing, they said, "go! Have a nice time". So that's what we did!' The SENCO-FORUM (2003b: 163) found that particularly for Key Stage 1 (seven-year-olds):

> Members felt that the SATs results did not tell them anything about the children's level of achievement which they did not know already. They were worried about the impact on children's self-esteem, and how this set the children back in their own progress. Furthermore, their knowledge of the children's personal experiences or family situations enabled them to notice when these affected their achievement.

This whole testing culture places an enormous amount of pressure on families and teachers, exacerbating the desire to recoil from difficulty and withdraw or exclude the child.

Some children themselves are excluded on the basis of their inability to interact with their mainstream peers. Marlene explained to me that Owen could not interact with the other children at the school 'because he didn't understand the rules' of games such as football 'and that ended up with the children turning on him'. Unfortunately one of these incidents resulted in Owen running to the toilets and locking himself in. Owen did have a welfare assistant, however the school did not make use of her to 'calm him down'.

> What they done was they sent the caretaker over the top of the toilet door which frightened him, grabbed him and as soon as he's been grabbed he's even worse, he's gone to bolt in the opposite direction and now they've got two caretakers and it ended up with him being restrained face down with his arms behind his back, with an adult male laying across his back and an adult male laying on his legs for an hour. And it was an hour before I was even called. They pinned him down. It took ten glasses of water to re-hydrate. He couldn't even stand he was in such a state. So we had a huge to do over that. At the end of the day he ended up with 25 hours support and he just really went from bad to worse. He couldn't cope.

Like Una and Katy, Marlene also stressed that the assistants should be trained, because her son

> would have tables and chairs overturned at just the slightest thing ... but they had their cues, but the person that was dealing with him wasn't trained, she was really like Mrs Bloggs from up the street which was the worst sort of person you could put with him.

This indicates that parents realise their children may not be receiving high-quality support when inclusive education promotes quality education for all, never mind the difficulty their children experience while negotiating the rules of mianstream schools.

Other parents highlight problems that occurred within the mainstream environment.

> I don't think he was coping very well at all, but because he couldn't express it ... he couldn't say anything he'd come home and he'd ... he'd be upset, it was a horrible time ...
>
> (Katy)

> It really isolates the child though. Because they've got the differences and there's no other children around the same, they don't fit anywhere, they're like a square peg in a round hole, they don't achieve because they're always at the bottom of the class ...
>
> (Tracy)

I'd say he's more withdrawn as the intensity of school has picked up.... He came home and the teacher had shouted at him and he's in the bottom group ... in that bottom group they are naughty, disruptive, bad manners, swearing and he was quite upset that he was in this group being branded with this ...

(Kim)

Based on Owen's difficult behaviour the head teacher did not want Owen back after the summer holidays. The LEA wanted him to go into a residential placement, but Marlene adamantly refused that option. He had no education from September through to November that year, until he finally received home tuition. Again, out of the mainstream environment, Marlene said, 'he came on in leaps and bounds with her, but at the same time although he was doing well educational wise, socialising he'd taken a huge leap backward because he'd been isolated really ...' After a struggle Marlene got him back into the PRU, but by the time I interviewed her a second time, she was still looking for the most suitable placement for Owen's secondary education.

Marlene's as well as Merl's, Tracy's and Lynne's sons experienced a period at home where they received some education, as a result of exclusion from mainstream education. It is clear here that the more disruptive the behaviour of the child within the mainstream environment, the more likely they are to be excluded. However, where the child is educated (or not) can have a significant effect on his or her life chances. Some children's difficult behaviour is a result of poor socialisation and for others, as in this study, it is about the effects of an impairment such as AS or AD/HD. Saying that all difficult students are to be educated together is something that has to be seriously considered, as a child with AS may suffer in an equally inappropriate placement, for example, with children who have behavioural problems for a reason other than an impairment.

All of the above examples show that inclusive education and exclusion is not simply a matter of placement (see also Benjamin, 2002; Lindsay, 2003; McDonnell, 2000; Norwich, 2000 and Wilson, 1999). Mainstream education for many of the parents and their children is not an easy or straightforward path. Based on the stories in this study, a move from contradictions within policy directives, and conflicts between them, about including children with impairments in mainstream schools and the privileging of academic achievement is necessary. Broadly speaking, think about how within the political and cultural spheres, the contradictions between bureaucratic systems of social control, and the socio cultural patterns of inclusion and exclusion have developed.

## Marlene's exclusionary experience

For a handful of parents in this research, the isolation and exclusion of themselves in the playground and their children's exclusion from parties and playtime has led to feelings of humiliation, loneliness, anger and sadness experienced by both them and their perception of their child's exclusionary experiences. Owen was bullied because of his difficulties and Marlene told me about an incident that affected her when he was seven years old.

> The children had actually got him in the playground and thrown their dinners at him. Got him into a corner and throwing dirt, dinner whatever they could get their hands on. I had parents coming up to me ... I had one woman reduce me to tears in the playground. Well she actually said, 'are you Owen's mum?' I said, 'yes'. And I thought she was going to ask could he go round and play, 'cause at the age of seven he'd never ever been invited to a birthday party, erm ... he'd never been invited round anyone's house, he actually sent out party invitations and no one replied.

This describes Owen's treatment at the hands of the other children, but also conveys how desperate Marlene felt about how Owen was being treated, and her own exclusion in this episode.

Marlene talked to me repeatedly in the first interview about how she was treated by other parents of children in Owen's class. On one occasion a mother walked up to her in the playground and Marlene recalled,

> 'I just want you to know', she said, 'that I've asked the teacher that I don't want my child sitting anywhere next to your child', erm ... she said, 'I think he's mental, don't think he should be in this school with normal children ... I think you must be a single parent', she said, 'that must be why your child is so unruly'.... 'Some of the other parents might get together and ask ... we want him out of the school so we're going to boycott the school'.

Later on in that same interview she told me again about how this exclusion made her feel and how she wrote a poem about the experience.

> I wrote a poem about being in the playground ... I mean 'he wasn't sent a Christmas card because he's only fit to be loved by me' ... but it goes through like being alone, I felt so alone and so isolated.

The poem goes on to talk about how the other mothers who whisper and talk about how she is 'the mother of the little beast'.

Gray (2002: 742), in his study of the effects of stigma on parents of children with high functioning autism (or AS) in Australia, recognises that the parents have bad experiences both with the school authorities and others, especially in relation to their children who have EBD. In his research a mother tells of her experience.

> I suppose with the other parents at the school I feel a bit odd. With the parents of normal kiddies I feel, I don't know, like looked down on a bit, that sort of feeling ... it bothers me.

Gray goes on to say that the parents have difficulties because of the aggressive behaviour and that

> [t]he problem with aggression is particularly difficult in school, where some of the children in the study experienced frequent conflicts with teachers or fellow students without disability. In several cases, these problems had resulted in violent outbursts and led to suspensions and expulsions. For their part, the parents are the ones who are placed in the role of the mediators between their children and educational administrators who have a responsibility to maintain order and protect the safety of the other students.
>
> (ibid.: 745)

Another mother in his research explains, 'there are days when I fall apart. Towards the end of last year at school, I've left school in tears ... I mean that sort of thing happens quite often and you try to shut it out and distance yourself from it' (ibid.).

There does seem to be a clear pattern of dealing with practical difficulties between those parents who have a child with intellectual impairments and those who have children with difficulties that include anti-social behaviour, not just aggressive behaviour but any culturally defined unacceptable behaviour such as 'inappropriate' touching or lack of awareness of social norms. However, both sets of parents have problems engaging with the authorities and education process. Educating a child with impairments is not simply a matter of inclusion but engagement with the whole aspect of the impairment, child, parents and difficulties incurred.

## Residential placement: respite or provision?

A third of the children in this study are attending, or have attended, residential specialist provision, and one mother (at the time of interview) is currently seeking a residential placement for her daughter. Some of the parents have agonised over whether or not they can let their child go to carers and educators, and for others it has been sheer relief or respite from difficulties based on certain impairments. Residential education, for parents, is not a finite discussion about where and how they wish their child to be educated, and parents may change their minds as the child gets older, and needs change, for both the child/teenager and possibly the family. LEAs, except as a last resort, or in certain circumstances, do not generally recommend residential provision, as it is expensive and does not adhere to inclusive policies. So if parents want residential provision for their child, they often have to fight for the funding of an out of county residential placement (Morris et al., 2003: 70).

When I began interviewing Kerry in early 2001 she was adamant that she wanted her sons to follow a mainstream education path. Yet by the time her son Gary was seven years old, in 2002, he was at a specialist residential school, and she was appealing to the LEA for the same placement for Ian, her youngest, who in 2003 gained his place at the same school. Like Kerry, I too had a change of heart with regard to my own daughter's education placement, which is illustrated here in a verbatim transcript of a conversation between another mother (Karen) and me.

In September of 2001 Karen and I were discussing the availability of post-16 education and whether she would consider a residential placement for her son. At that time my daughter was fourteen and a half years old and thoughts (or not) about residential placement were not far from my mind!

Karen: ... there's no other choice it's [the local school for children with SLD that goes up to 19 years] or nothing ...
Chrissie: Or residential?
Karen: Yes ... you see that's a kind of thing I don't toy with ... and I'm not sure ...
Chrissie: I mean my child's older than yours but I've had to ...
Karen: ... look at it?
Chrissie: Look at it, and I'm not prepared to at 16, it's too young ... maybe 18 ...
Karen: I was thinking exactly ...
Chrissie: Yes 'cause as far as I'm concerned my daughter in a way will say to me ... she will be able to say to me at 18 ...
Karen: What she wants to do?
Chrissie: To be honest I'm the sort of person that ... if I found a day college that was suitable ... and ...
Karen: ... yes ...

> Chrissie: ... and the right place I'd move. I would move.
> Karen: That's quite a consideration ...
> Chrissie: ... but that's three and a half years away ...

It is clear here that neither Karen nor I wanted to consider our children going to residential school then, and yet, like Kerry, 18 months later I positively saw it as the best option for my daughter's future. If she was going to gain independence both practically and emotionally I could see few other alternatives within the county. So much so I had to convince the LEA to fund the out of county placement. In thinking about residential provision it is not simply about the child, but also the parents and siblings.

Tracy had her concerns about her youngest son, Brad, very early on, but by the time he went to school his difficult behaviour had escalated in the mainstream environment *and* at home. It was affecting both her and his siblings. At the age of nine things had got so bad that the final time the police turned up at the school, Tracy told them she did not want to take Brad home. After that incident he was not allowed back into the school and remained at home for about four months. The LEA finally recommended a residential placement, and by this time Tracy positively wanted this option. She explained to me that when he was at school 'I used to dread him coming home. I used to think, "Oh God, Brad's coming home" because I knew it would all start'. When her son had gone off to residential school she added,

> all I wanted was some quality time with the others. So I'd devote my time to them all week and at the weekends they understand ... I mean they still say, 'oh for God's sake do something with Brad'.

Even though Tracy's son was at a residential school for children with EBD, he was still excluded from time to time and has, since the second interview, been referred on to a different residential school.

Tracy told me that if he continued to be excluded from these types of schools the next step was a

> lock-up type ... and he'll be there 52 weeks a year and it's up to me if I want him to come home at any point for a holiday.... So ... which I don't want, because that's prison!

Tracy is not the only mother in this research to have found living with her child traumatic at times, although she did not feel this about her oldest impaired son whom she describes as an 'easygoing' teenager.

Like Tracy, Una and Francis have described their experience of residential school as a positive relief. Una's son was in mainstream school until the age of eight and then she was advised that residential education might be an option. In response to this she explained,

> If I'm being honest about this ... there was a part of me who died, and there was a part of me that went whoopee! Because we were completely worn out and when I think of parents who have three and four kids like this. I don't know how they survive. It's horrendous, absolutely horrendous.

When Una's son went to the residential school for a four-day taster it was the first time she and her husband had been on their own 'together properly to do something we really want to do', since he was born. So unable did she feel to meet her son's needs at home, that even when her son changed schools at 11 (and the school was an inappropriate placement and caused him a great deal of stress) she felt unable to have him live at home. It took her a year to secure a referral to another more appropriate school.

Francis's son was in mainstream school until he was 11 years old. When he was 10 Francis started looking around for a residential placement. The LEA would not support this and so she began looking for an independent boarding school that would provide an education for him. Events prior to this had culminated in her son's behaviour deteriorating from him being carried home from school kicking and screaming to smearing faeces round his bedroom walls at home. Francis at one point took him back to the school and she recalled, the head teacher said,

> 'You can't leave him here like that', and I said, 'you fucking well watch me, goodbye'. They said, 'we suggest you'd be better off moving him to another school', and I said, 'exclude him, I want him excluded ... NOW!' And they wouldn't exclude him.

Francis wanted the exclusion because that would give her grounds to appeal for a residential placement if the school was unable to support her son. After this incident she began to look into residential schools further because she felt it was either her life or his. She would have to either give up work and devote herself to his needs or send him away. This is how she saw it.

> I'll have to jack in, give in gracefully and stay at home, and I thought 'no I can't do it. I just cannot ... I can't bear the thought of being stuck with him', so we had to look at alternatives.

Francis did find an independent school that took her son but this meant her husband and she had to work hard in order to pay the fees. They were continuing to fight with the LEA for support when I last spoke to her.

Some parents do not feel relief, or that they need respite, but in fact feel that their *child would benefit* from a residential school for his or her growth and development. Trisha has two sons identified with dyslexia; the oldest is severely effected. Like Francis, Trisha and her husband have spent thousands of pounds on private residential education. Her oldest son was in mainstream education until he was 13 years old. She described him as being very unhappy there and explained to me,

> He entered the juniors and that was the trigger factor. There was work on the blackboard he couldn't read it, he couldn't understand it, he was frightened by it. He would run home and I'd take him back to the school and the head would hold him and the secretary would hold him as I left the school ... he was screaming ... he couldn't even write his name.

And even though he finally received a statement, the implementation was unsatisfactory due to different supply teachers going into the school without knowledge of the children who are statemented in the class.

Trisha said that her son used to come home from school so frustrated that she was frightened he might hurt someone. The school psychologist advised her to buy him a punch bag to vent this frustration. All of this became too much for the family and they found him a residential school, where he started on his 13th birthday. Trisha told me she was mortified. Her son hated the residential placement and was often running away, added to this Trisha and her other son were left crying on the doorstep every Sunday evening, but his academic ability improved dramatically. The school closed down after her son had been there only two terms and Trisha looked for another residential school. However, her son decided that he would go to the local mainstream comprehensive which had an individual teaching unit, the very school he refused to go to a year before. He simply wanted to be at home, but importantly, he was able to recognise the decisions he was making were significant, for himself and the whole family. Not all impaired children are able to make those decisions for themselves.

## Conclusions

The main findings here are about how education provision is experienced for children with impairments according to the parents, whether in mainstream environment or another type of special unit or school. What is clear is that inclusive education policies and directives are in direct conflict with the testing and examination culture in the current mainstream environment. In a way the arguments that permeate inclusive education pale into insignificance when hearing what the parents in this research have to say about their special education experience. Significantly, Darlington (2004: 3), the president of nasen (the national association for special educational needs), suggests,

> Every child should feel safe, have friends and feel valued, and have the highest attainable expectations set for them. Parents should feel confident that the school will welcome their children and celebrate their uniqueness. Staff should be professionally supported with training so that they are confident in meeting an increasingly diverse pupil population in a positive way.

This quote illuminates what the parents in my study are striving for. Clearly, inclusion within the mainstream does not enter into the equation when a child is unable to cope with that environment and whether the parent, the teacher or the LEA exclude or transfer to an alternative seems irrelevant. The need for some parents to have time to themselves and with the rest of their family and therefore push for residential placement can be overwhelming when faced with acute difficulties. The relief that these mothers have felt when they finally are able to regain in their life, and the rest of the family's life, some kind of 'normality' is a reprieve.

Stella, Karen and Tim, for example, did not want their sons to go to a special school, but wanted mainstream, however, their children ended up in special schools. Both Tim's and Stella's experience of this has been positive. Karen on the other hand did not have the time or energy, based on the emotional and practical difficulties incurred, to follow any other chosen activity apart from that of the 'carer'. That said, it was also found that parents in situations like this often change their minds about their child's future and education placement, as in the case of Kerry whose oldest son went from mainstream to residential and her youngest from MLD provision to residential school. Kim is another example whose son went from mainstream comprehensive to residential college, and myself, whose daughter went from mainstream primary to MLD secondary and residential college. This chapter has not simply been about whether or not the child is best placed in residential, special or mainstream though.

It was found that children who are 'included' in a mainstream school often experience exclusion practically, intellectually and emotionally based on their differences and difficulties. This, as highlighted, is caused and compounded by a testing and examination structure, cultural ignorance and misunderstandings about difference and difficulty. Marlene's son, Owen, had experienced all of the above types of exclusion based on his difficulties. Furthermore, the parents too experience a type of exclusion based on others' expectations of what is 'normal' and their expectations for their child's education. This may be explicit in the case of Marlene who was ostracised in the playground and wrote the poem about her experience, and Tracy's very negative experience with the head teacher; or implicit whereby others use a patronising or sympathetic tone as with Tracy's story about the 'daffodil heads', Una and her son being the school 'disabled mascot' and myself when others suggest my daughter is personable and passive.

This chapter has shown that parents who have children with impairments can be as prejudiced and ignorant of others with children who have different impairments and difficulties, especially in the early days of the identification process and their own acceptance of the impairment. This has been highlighted by the findings above when some parents have been horrified at the special school placement based upon a repulsion of visible anti-social behaviour. Kerry did not consider either of her sons to be in the same impairment group as the children she viewed when wandering around an MLD school. Less explicitly Neil too did not want his son going to a school that had children who displayed anti-social behaviour. Both told me that they did not consider their children to be like 'that' and did not want their children emulating the behaviour.

Ultimately these arguments are not about inclusion and exclusion, but about acceptance of difference *and* difficulty, not of tolerance, and worse still, prejudice. Cultural attitudes towards difference, disability and mental ability are deep-seated, as shown by Shakespeare (1994), where aversions to physical impairment and visible differences as well as anti-social behaviour, such as dribbling and head banging, are found to be common. As reiterated here by Sibley (1995: 51), who unpacks the 'imperfect' and 'grotesque' in relation to exclusion suggests,

'The idea of society assumes some cohesion and conformity which create, and are threatened by, difference, although what constitutes a threatening difference has varied considerably over time and space' (ibid.: 69). However, in late modernity it seems that an aversion to the 'grotesque' and 'mentally impaired' has not changed dramatically. These cultural attitudes run alongside the desires, hopes and expectations of parents for their child's future and their parenting process.

# 6
# Living with Impairment

In the previous three chapters I have moved from birth and emotional and practical responses to discovering that a child has an impairment, through to negotiating a child's education journey, including dealing with professionals and public others. In the present chapter, the last of these substantive chapters, I would like to reveal to the reader *how* rearing a child with impairments can affect parents and other family members. The chapter is divided into five sections and will cover the following material.

The first section builds upon aspects of exclusion and isolation already highlighted in the previous chapter and discusses it in relation to the emotional and practical implications. The second section explores how the support (or lack of it) experienced by the main carer affects her or his emotional and practical life. It seems that social support is of paramount importance to mothers in their everyday life (Oakley, 1992), and I would suggest that this includes the support of the husband/wife/partner (depending on who the main carer is), other members of the family, both immediate and extended, and friendship networks. The section is about those relationships, how participants in this research negotiated them and how the impaired child impacted upon them.

The third section unpacks stories of depression and mental health related to the difficulties incurred during the childrearing process. Notably, almost half of the participants have taken either anti-depressants or beta-blockers for depression, anxiety or panic attacks; three felt suicidal and seven have had thoughts of desertion or harm towards their child. It is important to recognise that most of the difficulties raised here occurred during crisis points. Not all the participants used medication to overcome their depression (not all were depressed) and not all participants wanted to desert their children. Here I tell the stories of those who suffered from acute depression and thoughts of suicide or desertion, to those who found other outlets to vent their frustrations when powerlessness, anger and sadness were experienced.

The fourth section is about the siblings of the impaired child and how parents interpret their other children's anger, frustration and general well-being in relation to their impaired son or daughter. The fifth section ends the chapter with the life changing effects upon the main carer including his or her working life. She or he has either wanted to go out to work in order to retain his or her 'self'and/or gain some kind of respite or stayed at home to become a full-time *professional parent*, sometimes at the cost of a career elsewhere. This section documents and analyses these stories and concludes the chapter. However, the stories in this chapter are not chronological, and each story can feed into another.

## Exclusion and isolation as disabling

Avery (1999), Barnes et al. (1999), Beresford (1995), Gray (2002), Mactavish and Schleien (2004), Read (2000) and Tozer (1999) in their studies on disability suggest that there are problems of social isolation, exclusion and mobility for families with impaired children, and particularly mothers. I have already touched upon this social isolation and exclusion specifically dealing with aspects of exclusion in the school playground in the previous chapter. I would like to now look, more broadly, at wider experiences of social isolation. Most of the participants in my research talked about their day-to-day lives indicating that they were either terrified to go out or embarrassed about their child's impairment and often withdrew socially. Writing about children without impairments, Ribbens (1994: 89) found that '[c]hildren could therefore be potentially disruptive of the rules of social interaction, with *embarrassment as a sign of breakdown*, almost leading to withdrawal' [emphasis in original]. Imagine the effect when a child does have an impairment, and furthermore, when the parent seems unable to 'control' her or his child's behaviour. Highlighted here by Gray (2002: 739), '[m]ost commonly parents imagined that others were critical of their child-raising abilities, not accepting of them and made them feel embarrassed. The latter was the most common manifestation of felt stigma ...' and furthermore, '[p]arents frequently noted that others didn't invite them over to their homes for social occasions such as dinners or parties or, if they did, often didn't invite them back' (ibid.: 740).

Parents made reference to the embarrassing aspect of their child's impairment, which then had an impact on their going out and about. Much of this embarrassment is based on their impaired child's behaviour and on what the parents perceive or imagine others are thinking. These issues also tie in with the previous chapter's discussion on aversion to the 'grotesque' and 'impure' (Douglas, 1966) and socially 'inappropriate' behaviour (Sibley, 1995). Kim said that her son 'used to headbutt the wall when he lost his temper which was really embarrassing … and that stopped me going to some of the toddler groups because I was too embarrassed that he might do that'. Katy told me that it was in the supermarket her son would 'scream his head off' and continued, 'one time I was going down the aisle and I wished the floor would swallow me up because this woman looked at me'. It is clear that this experienced embarrassment and therefore isolation is based upon the parents' expectation of their child's behaviour (as well as others' reactions). However, Stella was not prepared to let others dictate to her where she could and could not go, and Tim told me that 'well he's very good … publicly … we don't have a problem … I mean we have some problems … he's a bit incontinent … we have got some problems, but by and large he's good'. The social importance of children's behaviour on mothers in general is great, and '[t]he acceptability of their children to other adults was a frequent concern', as one of the mothers (in Ribbens, 1994: 87) said, 'I want her to be popular and I lay there worrying that people don't like her' (ibid.). For this mother (without an impaired child) it was crucial that other mothers liked her child. For parents in my study their child is often the one who is singled out as a problem or talked about by other mothers.

Guidelines on social acceptability, manners and showing respect are frequently cited (ibid.), and two particular problems that yet a child with impairments such as ASD may not be able to negotiate such social norms. Many of the parents in this study made direct reference to the fact that their impaired children did not get invited to parties because of their anti-social behaviour, as Marlene suggested in the previous chapter. And, a mother of a disabled child in Read's (2000: 99) research says,

> People think of our children as something separate – when they think of them at all. They're not ever in the same category as those who've had a dramatic accident and become paralysed … because you see, they were once 'real' people, and that's what makes the difference. If you were never 'real' then you're best forgotten.

This suggests that people with *intellectual* impairments are not real enough to have a part in mainstream society, let alone be included as fully fledged human beings, which theoretically takes us back to asking questions about what it is to be human (Swift, 1967 [1726]).

Una said that her son was inappropriately aggressive, which meant he was often socially excluded. 'He had major problems with intonation and reflection, and he can be very inappropriately aggressive and he doesn't mean to be, he just doesn't understand that he's doing it'. Francis and Merl also told me their sons were not invited to parties, 'the whole class would go except for Mark' (Francis), and Merl said, 'we were very isolated, very very isolated. Other people ... whose parents didn't want anything to do with our children because [our son] was displaying so many different oddities. ...' These mothers felt isolated and sad for their children, but some parents intentionally withdrew from certain social situations. Kim told me that she found nowhere to belong 'and so I think what I did was I withdrew a little bit from normal situations ... toddler groups ... where mums would notice'. Isolation and, at worst, imprisonment in the home were not only about others' reactions and self-withdrawal. Exclusion was also about the actual impairment causing distress and potential danger.

For some impaired children with heightened sensory perception, or little social, perceptual or spatial awareness, the social world can be a frightening and potentially dangerous place. It seemed that some children did not feel pain in the usual sense and some were a danger to themselves and others. Mary told me that she did not want to be out with her son because of his reactions and explained,

He just couldn't cope with it ... he went through increased anxiety when we left the house, increased stimulus awareness almost so he became bombarded by it ... obvious because he'd close his eyes and have his hands over his ears when we went out. We couldn't go to the market. He couldn't cope with crowds.

Neil commented on the 'disabled family' and said,

we didn't function as a family, I mean ... you've probably heard that a lot, you know, if you've got a disabled child ... it's not the child that's disabled, it's the family and for a long time we didn't do things ...

Before his son came along, the family used to go swimming, but since then Neil was worried about his son's health and welfare and said that they did not go swimming because 'he would jump on his knees until his knees used to bleed and he had no sense of pain'. Neil also told me that he was frightened to take his son out because

> we can't erm … really take him out into the public because he was a danger to himself, he'd run out in the roads if you didn't hang onto him. You couldn't put reins on him because he'd just scream … he'd just scream all the time. He didn't relate to anybody, he was in his own world most of the time.

Tracy saw the danger in her son's behaviour, but feared for others too because he 'was throwing bricks through people's windows as you walked past … if I hadn't been level-headed I'd have thought he was possessed'.

What this section highlights is the isolating impact and restrictions placed on the social activities of the family and, specifically, the main carer. She or he is unable to engage fully within mainstream society without either feeling that she or he is compromising on her or his duty as a mother or father and is likely to feel responsible for being unable to control her or his child's behaviour, or simply that she or he does not belong by being ostracised. It is clear that the parents often need support that goes beyond ordinary support expected of and from partnerships, family and friendship networks. The following section documents the support mothers and fathers have experienced, or not, as the case may be.

## Support as a foundation of well-being

One of the most important issues discussed by many of participants in this research is the level of experienced support. Support in this study is based on a perception or *expectation* of support. It is about whether or not the mother or father feels supported by his or her partner, family or friendship networks (formal or informal). I would suggest that this level of support has a very positive effect upon the mother's or father's mental health and general well-being when going through stressful periods. In my own case, I have experienced support from my mother and the wider family and as a single parent. As a result of this support I was able to work outside the home part-time, study part-time and negotiate my daughter's difficulties. My sister took my daughter in every evening and cared for her, which was the most important thing. My mother was also a tower of strength, and I have been lucky to have an extended supportive family, including my daughter's paternal grandparents.

Why this is pivotal when talking about whether the family is affected or, in fact, disabled by their child's impairments, is that the support a mother or father may feel they have from those family members and friends, often impacts upon their coping mechanisms, emotional security and practical autonomy. Not experiencing support can paralyse mothers and fathers, rendering them disabled both emotionally and practically. Oakely (1992: 39), in *Social Support and Motherhood*, suggests that the more support a mother can have, especially in times of crisis or ill health, the more positively it will affect her health.

1. Social support affects health directly.
2. Social support improves health by acting as a buffer to stress.
3. Social support makes stress less likely.
4. Social support facilitates recovery from illness or crisis.

However, she also suggests that these relationships are not simply about cause and effect. Phillipson et al. (2004) suggest that there are both 'anti-social' and 'not anti social' aspects to social networks. It could be argued that this is the case for parents in this research and other 'disabled' networks, as some networks can be broadly exclusive and divisive, while being supportive at a local level.

Tozer (1999: 16) in her research on 24 families with two or more severely impaired children found that although these families express the same emotions as any other family

> [w]here there are two or more disabled children, their relationships with other family members can be very different [...] and affects everyone in the family requiring time and attention from the whole household and often those in the wider family too.

Furthermore, Beresford (1995: 21) in her research of 1100 families with severely impaired children found that '[t]he majority of respondents in our survey who were married, or living as married, received high levels of practical and emotional support from their partners. Nevertheless one in five said they received only a little help from their partner'.

Baldwin and Carlisle (1999: 347) in their research discovered, when looking at the Office of Populations and Census Surveys (OPCS) on disability, that 'more than half of the parents in this study reported that having a disabled child had *not* affected their marriage. Another 45 per cent said it *had* ...' (emphasis in original). Emerson (2003: 385–99) in a large-scale study in the UK sampled 245 mothers who had disabled

children and 9481 who did not. With regard to the mother–father relationships, Emerson found that for those mothers who had children
with impairments, an equal number had reported that their relationship with their partner had either weakened or strengthened, implying
an effect, whether it was positive or negative. More often than not the
parents describe the support not in practical terms, but in being *emotionally supported* based on *expectation* of support, validation of emotions
and recognition of difficulties.

### The importance of *feeling* supported

Just under a third of the parents in this research felt supported by the
father or mother of their child (or in the case of Trinny, a single parent,
by her mother). Significantly, apart from Trinny, all of those who felt supported were married. Katy and Trisha had traditional expectations of their
roles within the family, and when asked about support, Katy's husband
said, 'we knew from very early on, for us to get the best for [our son] we
would have to work and be united'. Katy added, 'But we are with the rest
of the family. We do make a stand together, don't we?' (as she looked to
her husband for confirmation, he agreed). Trisha reiterates this even
though she did much of the 'care-work'. She said that her husband
worked long days, but as she spoke about what she had done for her
oldest son with regard to his impairment needs she remembered,
'I mean bearing in mind I'm saying it's all me! My husband was battling
with us as well, but he worked [Laughs]. He didn't have the time'. She
went on to say that her husband did feel guilty about her doing much
of the 'work' because

> you've got one partner trying to do everything. I have to say we're a
> Christian family, so an awful lot of prayer went on [...] but no, we
> did it together. But I often did meetings [to do with her son's educa-
> tion] on my own because [my husband] couldn't get off work.

Significantly, although she may have spent much of her time going to
official meetings, 'caring' and 'researching' on her own, importantly,
she still felt supported. This seems fundamental when looking at mothers'
or fathers' mental health, as illustrated in the next section.

With regard to feeling unsupported, only one of the seven parents
remained married. Tracy felt unsupported since the birth of her twin
boys. She told me that she had to learn medical and nursing techniques

and that David needed more support than would usually be expected and, therefore, needed additional support for herself.

> I think David's dad resented the less time I had for him. ... you get up in the night and you feed one and as you put one down the other's waking and you'd be up ... David would take up to an hour to take a bottle so I'd be up for a three-hour stint in the night. Now his dad at the time wasn't working and he didn't get up, and I resented that. ... He'd always lay there and you knew he was awake but he's says oh I didn't hear them. When you've got two babies you can't help but hear!

Feeling supported or unsupported in any relationship depends on the parents' own interpretation of what support means to them. The parents in this study who experienced support described it not in tasks and practical support, so much as being emotionally supported and experiencing a validation of their expectations.

Jack, who started out as a full-time manual worker with his wife taking the main responsibilities for the care of their children, told me that things changed when he became convinced that all was not well at home. Out of their three sons the oldest and the youngest, both, had MLD. He said in the early days he thought that his first son was a 'late developer'. 'I did not realise that she [his wife] was keeping all of them in nappies far too long. ... She wasn't encouraging them to get out of nappies'. Jack told me that his oldest was not out of nappies until he was six or seven years old. In 1995 when the youngest was nine (who at the time was still in nappies), Jack took over the main care of all three sons. 'I virtually took over in '95. She became mentally ill and I took the children ... she was finding it difficult to control them'. The situation for Jack came to a head when a child protection team became involved when their oldest son went to school bleeding after being bitten by his mother. Jack never felt supported by his wife and yet he indicates that she may have had some mental health difficulties and even suggests he was not sure if she might have had some learning difficulties. Once the relationship broke down, his wife only had supervised access. Ultimately Jack expected his wife to care for their children based upon his expectations of what a mother's role was, and yet when he discovered that she was not coping he felt disappointed.

There were eight participants who felt unsupported but *became* supported via a change in expectation often based on a change in the relationship. Six of these were still married to the father of their impaired child. Kerry separated from her husband during the research and found it quite hard coming to terms with motherhood, as both she and her husband had led lives as a childless married couple for nine years. Her first son was difficult and eventually was diagnosed with verbal dyspraxia. Kerry told how she felt unsupported both practically and emotionally based on her expectations of her husband's role, as she described an event that took place at a children's birthday party. We have already seen part of this narrative in Chapter 1, but it is important to revisit it here because it describes the way Kerry experiences her husband's support, or the lack of it.

> [My husband's] way of dealing with it was to push it out of the way and not look at it ... he left a tremendous amount for me to deal with ... for example, when we went to a birthday party a little girl got scratched on the eye, quite badly actually, Gary really did scratch her and erm ... the mother went absolutely berserk, and I was standing there trying to reason with her and say 'you know I'm really sorry' and 'my son has a speech and language problem and he can't hear very well ... and he has a problem with children around him' and she was saying things like 'well that's not my problem that's yours'. Then I discovered I was struggling at this point trying to fight back the tears, trying to be in control, bearing in mind there were about 30 people standing around me all silent and her screaming at me and erm ... *to discover my husband was standing behind me* ... I think that was a turning point for me ...

Kerry was disappointed and angry that her husband did not intervene on her behalf, or, at the very least, support her in this situation. Various episodes of unsupportive incidents and a general lack of emotional support led to the eventual demise of their relationship. However, after the break-up Kerry and her husband now support each other with both their sons' education, official meetings and social events. Significantly, the difference for her now is that she no longer *expects* the emotional support in the same way as when they were a couple and therefore feels more supported.

Although none of the parents who are divorced or separated have suggested that the difficulties they experienced with their impaired child caused the breakdown of the relationship, some have indicated that the difficulties of the child brought to the fore difficulties in their relationship that may not have arisen had the path been somewhat smoother. Stella stressed, 'Nathan's challenges didn't help, but they weren't really the main cause of the problems that my husband and I had'.

Babs suggested to me that her husband 'spent a lot of years in denial about what Ben's problem was [...] I dealt with the kids in many ways. All the emotional stuff [...] as well as the practical things'. She told me that eventually, due to all the stresses and strains of their son's impairments and the 'work' she was doing, as well as the fact that her husband was made redundant, they separated. Her husband got a job in another area and he left. However, time apart and, again as with Stella's husband, spending time with their son alone during access weekends made him 'realise what we're dealing with and what it felt like ...' Babs and her husband got back together after two years and she told me, 'we were stronger when we got back together, and I think the experience my husband had of being on his own with Ben was quite crucial ...' This narrative suggests that Ben did have a part to play in the breakdown of her relationship (although many parents deny this). Other research also suggests having an impaired child can impact negatively upon a relationship (see Baldwin and Carlisle, 1999 and Beresford, 1995).

## Support beyond the relationship

Support is not simply an experience between the father and mother. It is clear that not all parents remain in their relationship but still feel supported in some capacity. Out of the 24 parents interviewed, 20 said that they had experienced support through either family and or friends who were not part of the immediate family unit or support groups. *Expectation* is an important part in thinking about how support and difficulty is experienced, perceived and ultimately lived with.

Tim, a middle-aged father, felt supported by his wife, but did not expect support from outside the family. Tim did not feel he needed any more support other than from his wife and, as I said, did not expect it. He told me that he had friends, but expressed, 'no, I wouldn't regard friends as much of support really. But I don't expect them ... to be honest'. This expectation of support, or not, is crucial in how the mother/father may be affected by their support networks. Kerry, on the other hand, felt that her friends *should* be supportive, but felt unsupported because of the way she felt perceived by them.

I didn't feel that there were a lot of friends that did understand erm. ... and I think that they thought we weren't disciplining them, erm ... we did have one set of friends that were excellent and really stood by us and have been a tremendous support and probably always will be ... but of course we lost a lot of friends because of it. Nobody wants their child to be hit and scratched and punched by another child.

The 'lack of support' Kerry experienced outweighed, to a certain extent, any support she received and she therefore felt unsupported most of the time, which caused her great emotional anxiety. Kerry found it very hard to come to terms with both her sons' impairments and this is reflected in how she experienced support (or lack of it) and her mental well-being.

Coming to terms with an impairment can take longer for some, and part of this process is about the denial of the severity of the impairment, as described in Chapter 3. In my own case I denied the severity of my daughter's impairment by avoiding support groups and contact with other parents of impaired children. Mothers in this research have expressed similar feelings as revealed here:

> I've never wanted to socialise with parents of children who have difficulties. And I think that is really to do with the fact that I haven't wanted to accept my children's problems. As far as I'm concerned they are totally normal and even now I have people saying to me 'oh my god, how do you cope?' and I don't know any different!
>
> (Kerry)

> I've had times when I've felt really down ... yeah I went to a couple of sessions [support group] where I sat with people who'd got special needs wringing their hands and I thought this is not me. This makes me feel worse rather than ... I've got a good support network in close friends ... and without being ... sounding totally selfish I don't want to invest too much energy in hearing other people's problems.
>
> (Trinny)

> There was this support group ... but it was so depressing, I only went once. I thought I'm not ever going there ... it was absolutely awful. It was called family support or something and I thought I don't need this support ... in this tiny little room full of all these mothers moaning.
>
> (Karen)

> I was told there was a support group at the children's centre ... and I would have run a mile as I just didn't want to know ... erm ... a couple of notices about things that you don't want to face basically, you know, poems about how 'special' children are a 'gift from God' ... I thought 'no they're not!' [Laughs] I thought I don't want to sit around talking to other people about things like that, I really don't. Because that was the last thing I felt, and that sort of holy attitude and these 'little gifts' that we've all got to care for, I couldn't handle that at all.
>
> (Babs)

Nevertheless, these parents often change their minds when they have come to terms with the impairment. More significantly, they have put a label on the impairment, as later on in our interview Babs told me that she 'now runs a support group for Asperger families'. Although not explicit in the interview it is implied that this is a proactive group, and is something different from 'sharing sob stories', however, a support group all the same. Much of this support is based on where the mother or father is in their journey of coming to terms with their child's impairment. The narratives above seem to imply that there is an element of 'tragedy' in the support group network they experienced, or at the very least they believe there to be one, and one which they do not want to be involved in.

In Beresford's (1995: 22) study, she says, 'less than a third of parents in our sample belonged to a support group, and a similar proportion had chosen not to belong to a group'. Just over a third in my smaller sample have been involved in support groups, yet my sample is biased towards those parents who may be more likely to attend support groups due to my initial point of contact. Similar to mine, in Beresford's (1995: 23) study the parents' reason for going to the support groups was a 'chance to talk to other parents ... being able to exchange information about benefits, local services, the child's condition and ways of meeting future needs'. Oakley (1992: 29) reiterates this when she says, '[n]etworks provide shared norms, values and ideologies'. To illustrate what Beresford implies about exchanging information and future needs, Lynne, once she had a diagnosis of AS (which did not happen until her son was 14 years old), told me,

> I joined the Asperger's group ... and spoke to other parents and they'd said if you want a specialist college you're going to have to start doing the research ... so I did all that, and I found one I wanted, erm ... all sort of fitted him quite well.

Lynne used the group as a point of information gathering. She wanted to know what happens next and how to move forward in procuring the best possible future for her son by learning from experiences other mothers have.

Like Lynne, Mary too found the support group to be a useful resource based on other parents' past experiences.

> So I had a support of people who had been there before me in similar circumstances and the autistic spectrum group in [name] is excellent. Excellent people, all the legal knowledge and I did get a lot of help there.

However, the support group is not simply about resource and practical advice as other mothers have said. Stella found her support network via the special needs school and coffee mornings. She told me that a mother who has a child with impairments needs an outlet with other mothers who can relate to each other and have a common understanding. She made her close friends as a result of her networks and commented,

> I think that I am so lucky that I have such wonderful friends in the school, that I wouldn't have met if I hadn't had Nathan ... I've got a very close friend who's got a son with autism and what she goes through ... and we talk to each other and we ... if people could hear us! We laugh about the most awful things that are so horrendous [we laugh] and if you don't laugh we'd be down the bottom all the time. Even though ... what we say is that our children are so different that it doesn't mean her challenges are worse than mine, they're just different. I think that's the important thing to remember really.

This implies that laughing and being able to share the messy stories, and not always in a way one would do with others outside of the group, for fear of seeming uncaring, can have an immensely cathartic effect.

Sometimes simply having someone who can empathise with the mother/father has resulted in experiencing support, and as with Stella, Christine has made friends via these networks and explained,

> [My group] was useful and other parents were saying the same thing 'oh I'm having trouble getting my child to use the potty' and 'oh I'm glad I'm not the only one!' That kind of thing ... I met this woman who I see about once a month ...

For those mothers who find this kind of support and networking useful it has clearly had a positive effect on their lives and aided the 'official' process too, lessening the long-term disabling impact. For example, as discussed in chapters 4 and 5, if there are legal loopholes a support group can often be a space to discuss and learn about such issues.

Read (2000: 56) in her research found that mothers who do not have disabled children rely on informal support networks such as 'reciprocal childcare and babysitting arrangements' and that this 'may not be readily available to the mother of a severely disabled child'. Barnes et al. (1999: 102) have also found that '[t]he effects of having a disabled child on family life depend on the family's existing relationships and circumstances, with some able to draw on more resources and support than others'. When talking to parents in this research about their support, it was found that although many have experienced support from family/friends and support groups, likewise they have also felt unsupported, and at times excluded. Baldwin and Carlisle (1999) have found that there are emotional (effects on mental health), practical (effects of career/home work and public restrictions) and financial costs in bringing up an impaired child. Mactavish and Schleien's (2004) research on 65 families with impaired children focussed on recreation and aspects of family life that draw out the impacts of what Baldwin and Carlisle (1999) would call 'practical costs', for example, restricted socialisation. Mactavish and Schleien (2004) found that there were negative impacts upon the families as they often had to plan well in advance allowing for little spontaneity, be organised, and often fewer members of the family were involved based on differing needs.

Public or explicit exclusion and rejection adds to these already difficult experiences. As we have already discovered Kerry 'lost' friends who did not understand her difficulties, and Marlene was ostracised in the playground. A quarter of the parents talked openly about how ordinary networks or friendships had been tested when an impaired child entered the family as illustrated here. Both Neil and Tracy lost their babysitting arrangements, thereby disabling them socially.

> People would say, 'I'll take the girls off your hands ...' yeah, but there's one more. Yeah but there's very few people who would want to look after our son. Understandably because they just would not know how to cope.
>
> (Neil)

Tracy did not experience support for either son, for different reasons. The oldest one had medical problems, which meant Tracy had to learn nursing skills ... '[b]ut nobody offered because I think they were all too frightened to. Because they'd all witnessed me doing all the bits and bobs with him ...' With her youngest son, support was not forthcoming because of his anti-social behaviour, for example, as we have already heard, when Brad threatened to kill the babysitter. Clearly the lack of support is both at an emotional level and at a practical level, rendering the parents actually disabled, isolated and excluded from certain activities.

This section has demonstrated that support for parents of an impaired child is crucial. The support of a partner, it seems, has a positive effect on the general well-being of the mother or main carer, but significantly, so too do other forms of support, such as family and friendship networks as well as support groups. However, feeling supported is more important in dealing with the emotional and practical effects. Support groups, especially before the parent has come to terms with the impairment, do not necessarily have a positive impact and therefore are generally not sought after initially. However, if an impairment is identified and labelled, and subsequently the appropriate support group identified (rather than a generic disability group), it seems parents are more likely to attend and gain support. I would suggest that this is down to specific knowledge (of the impairment) feeding into a significantly empowered position. In the following section this documented support is analysed in more detail with regard to the mothers' and fathers' mental health.

## Depression, anxiety and mental health

Many parents do not talk about how bad they feel because of social pressures on what it is to be a 'good mother' (Hollway and Featherstone, 1997; Ribbens, 1994; Silva, 1996). Parker (1997: 17) goes as far as to say that mothers often cover up being 'enraged, entranced, embattled, wounded and delighted by their children' through the safety of comic accounts of maternal ambivalence in magazines, newspapers and novels. However, mothers and fathers with an impaired child have found it harder to hide some of these feelings, and yet felt guilty for being depressed and possibly wanting to desert or harm their child.

Depression and mental health difficulties seem to be under-researched for mothers and fathers of children with learning impairments. Baldwin and Carlisle (1999: 342) in their research on families and disabilities talk about the 'costs' of parenting an impaired child, which include financial, practical and emotional costs.

> The emotional stresses reported in the literature include many centring on the child and her condition – anxieties about illness, death, what will happen when she grows up. They centre, often, on milestones not reached and on transitional phases – starting school, adolescence or school leaving age. They also extend to worries about effects on other children and on partners. The hard practical work and the isolation resulting from restriction on social life and from restrictions on employment is clearly a potential source of emotional strain ...

They also suggest that parents of impaired children are likely to experience higher levels of stress, as does Beresford (1995). Read (2000: 48) found that 10 out of the 12 mothers who took part in her research 'spoke of the substantial stress and anxiety that this had caused them at various times'. Morgan (1996: 105) highlights the intensity and complexities of emotional labour when caring for a sick child, and that the mother often has to draw on her emotional resources while also trying to control them.

I agree with Baldwin and Carlisle (1999) that much research, including mine, does concentrate on what will happen to the child – education, major transitions and milestones, in relation to the parents – because that is what the mothers/fathers generally talk about. However, in my research, when the mothers/fathers talked about their stress and anxieties, I encouraged them to talk a little more about this (if they were able to). I wanted to know how this stress and anxiety manifested, what they did about it and what some of the feelings and emotional impacts were. None of the parents in my research said that their emotions remained stable during particularly difficult periods. Almost half had taken either anti-depressants or beta-blockers for depression or panic attacks, three told me they had felt suicidal and seven had thoughts of either harming or deserting their child. Significantly, out of the nine parents who felt and experienced support none were on anti-depressants. This suggests that experiencing support has a positive impact on the mothers' mental health, especially during times of acute stress.

Feelings of desertion and harm to a child in many cases would be thought of as a serious mental health problem and warrant surveillance of the child and the family by the state in case of injury, yet Parker (1997: 17) on mothering in general suggests that

> [n]one of us find it easy to truly accept that we both love and hate our children. For maternal ambivalence constitutes not an anodyne condition of mixed feelings, but a complex and contradictory state of mind, shared variously by all mothers, in which loving and hating feelings for children exist side by side.

I would argue that this love/hate dualism is even more apparent for mothers and fathers of an impaired child because in late modern society parents are told 'how to' rear children (Furedi, 2001), and that, fundamentally, is about caring for and meeting the needs of their children. However, if a child is impaired she or he will require additional care. The mother or father cannot necessarily meet all of her or his needs.

Karen is divorced and felt unsupported, but did not take any medication for depression, even though she felt depressed and had an acute feeling of hate for her son, and on one particularly bad day said to social services, 'I'm going to kill him'. Karen could not cope with all her children together because of Kevin's aggressive behaviour towards his siblings. She was unable to have a 'normal' relationship with them while he was around. However, after a 'night off', she was able to recoup her energies. Francis, like Karen, told me that she has 'disliked Mark intensely', and did not want to be at home with him. However, Francis also said to me she would talk to her mum and sister about her difficulties and found this a better 'therapy' than anything the doctor could give her.

Mary, Kerry, Tracy and Neil, all in one way or another admitted 'desertion', or had thoughts of desertion, acute in the early days. All four of them had spells on anti-depressants. Both Neil and Kerry 'deserted' their families for a period of time, and Kerry and Tracy said they felt suicidal at times. Neil 'deserted' the family, initially by drinking and turned down the offers of anti-depressants.

> I mean I went to the doctor about it and he said 'well I could offer you these' and I just wanted to freak out 'NO! I can't do this; I can't ...' silly really maybe I should have gone for it. Maybe it would have helped me get through my depression quicker, I don't know. To me it's like no matter what drug I take I've still got the problem to deal with at the end of it. ... But I've always liked to drink, but I went heavy at it... I hated coming home ... I hated going to work ... you just chuck something down your neck and forget about it all.

However, when I carried out a follow-up interview a year later Neil continued to have difficulties with the processes that surround assessment and his son's impairments. He had six months off work due to stress and told me that he could not cope any more. He had stopped drinking as much, but was taking anti-depressants and told me that he had 'come back' into the family.

Kerry 'deserted' her family, and at more than one point told me she wanted to die. Kerry said that she was on anti-depressants for a year and then came off them but went back on them because she could not cope. She explained,

> I was near to breakdown. When I couldn't stop crying I did go to the doctors and he said you are on the verge of a breakdown ... I think at one point the easier thing would have been to die. I thought I was a crap mother, I'm going off doing this course, that everyone says I'm a crap mother and I don't love my husband anymore.

Her way of coping with the stress in the early days was to remove herself physically and go to college and stay away from the home as much as possible.

> For a while I walked away from my children, because I couldn't emotionally deal with their problems and that was very hard for me because I've never walked away from them ... but I did. And I let [my husband] do it and I said to him 'you deal with it' ... I walked away from it. I stayed out of the house as much as I possibly could; I let him pick them up, although I dropped them off and did the usual thing, but when it came to the emotional things I let him deal with it. And I don't know whether that was a good thing or a bad thing, all I know is that I had to do that to keep my marbles. I would have just lost it otherwise ... I think my subconscious mind knew that I was getting to a point where I couldn't handle them and I didn't want to let rip and then part of me was angry ... and you're the father and you haven't ... and now you do it because I'm not strong enough, so you can do it whether you like it or not. I lost a lot of friends, I completely cut myself off ... I thought it was easier to stay away ... I did not want to hear whether I was doing the right thing or the wrong thing.

This excerpt is hugely revealing in the emotional roller coaster between managing emotions and doing what she thought was right. Kerry realised that in order to cope she had to remove herself. Had she not, she was concerned that she might harm herself or her children. However, the supportive words of one friend helped Kerry enormously. On the morning of a particularly black day Kerry wanted 'to take a bottle of pills', but that morning she received a phone call from a friend who told her, 'you're a fantastic mother, and where you've got your dedication from and courage I'll never know'. Kerry responded very positively to this phone call and said, 'it meant so much to me, and I thought someone noticed when I felt no one had'. What can be seen here is that Kerry felt totally alone and the work that she carried out as a mother, for example, with the professionals, went unnoticed, she felt unsupported by her husband and thought she was a bad mother.

Tracy too had reached breaking point because Brad had been excluded from school and had broken the law, and she too thought she was a bad mother.

> I was at breaking point ... and I'd been to the doctors and I was on anti-depressants. Erm ... a couple of times I thought about taking

the lot of them and a big bottle of booze and just finishing it all ... I'd had enough ... I was gonna be either insane ... erm... or top meself. I couldn't do it any more ... everyday I got up scared of what the day would bring ... I got to the stage where I thought I was a completely lousy mother and they'd be better off without me anyway ... if I wasn't around.

And the final straw for Lynne was when her son was suspended for inappropriate sexual behaviour. She told me, 'I was just about suicidal ... I was desperate, I just did not know what to do ... he was suspended for touching girls at school'.

Of the 11 parents who did not have medication for depression, eight were married to the father of their impaired child; one was remarried and experienced support from him. Another was a single parent but her mother helped out, and the other parent was Jack, who was divorced. It did not occur to him to get support from others during his particularly stressful time. It is these parents who were less likely to feel depressed. Kim said that she had the support of her sisters, and Katy told me she and her husband were 'united together'; Trisha felt supported by her husband but also said that her Christian faith had helped her. 'If I didn't have that then maybe I would have gone to the doctors for help, but I didn't feel I needed to'. Kat referred to her 'close knit family' when asked about support. Whereas Christine and Tim displayed a more pragmatic and positive attitude to their situations as indicated here:

> I would have thought that's how I'd react but I think I've spent very little time crying about it because there's no point, you know he is what he is ... whatever he is you can't make them into something ... I thought this was the one I'm going to enjoy the most. I didn't realise he'd be a baby for so long ... well not a baby but ...
>
> (Christine)

> It's like getting over a bereavement, it's gradual. ... But gradually you become, I mean now he's 16 and you just become ... a lot of the time you just get used to the fact that he's just our son and you don't bother on the day-to-day basis.
>
> (Tim)

The parents' stories have illustrated experiences of stress, depression and anxiety that have had a dramatic effect on their mental health. This in turn affects the family as a whole, and often at crisis points disables the family as a unit. It is here I would like to follow on with the effects on the siblings of the impaired child.

## Siblings and their impaired brother or sister

The above kind of emotional activity based on disappointment, denial and lack of support, the time spent on the child with impairment, added to the social restrictions expressed by many of these families, has had a dramatic disabling effect on the siblings of the impaired child, this is evident in other research (Carpenter, 2000; Read, 2000; Seligman and Darling, 1997 and Warren Dodd, 2004). Seligman and Darling (1997: 118–44) indicate that such siblings often experience a level of responsibility that goes beyond their years, that they demonstrate anger and resentment towards the parents and/or the impaired child and sometimes even their basic life goals are affected, based on their interaction with their impaired sibling.

Read (2000: 27) in her research suggests that non-disabled children need to have explanations. She pointed out that one of her mothers said,

[s]ometimes Emily says to me, 'if I'd done that, you'd have been angry with me'. I say to her, 'you have to stop and think how Louise's life is compared with yours. She can't just get up and do something like you can'.

She went on to explain that another mother told her, '[i]t was tough. All your energies seem to go on one child and I think Louise missed out a bit at that time. She says now she remembers and she resented all the attention [her brother was getting]' (ibid.). Warren Dodd (2004: 42) indicates that some of the problems encountered by siblings include limited time and attention from parents, concerns about bringing friends home, stress in the home, embarrassment about the impaired sibling and restrictions on family outings. By setting up group work specifically for the siblings, she 'confirmed the value of work with siblings of your children with disabilities. These young people have needs of their own which require attention, understanding and support' (ibid.: 48). The siblings' care and attention (or lack of) from their mother or father, the impaired child's anti-social behaviour, loss of outings as a family and, for some, loss of material goods can be disabling.

For siblings, the reasons as to why their brother or sister might behave differently, and their mother or father treat them differently, may not always be understood. Neil's description of what he recalled illustrates his daughters' difficulties in coming to terms with their brother's problems.

> Like the girls ... seeing one of my daughters crying ... and I said, 'what's the matter?' 'I'm sad because Kane isn't like other boys', or 'I'm sad because Kane's got problems'. 'I'm sad because he won't come to our school', so yeah it's affected them ... I mean one of the saddest things is we were given this figure ... what's it called? Something that you'd put on the telly or mantel piece ... a bit of art work, and it obviously had two parents and a child and [my daughter] said 'oh look it's mummy and daddy and Kane', and I thought, 'oh flippin' 'eck', they almost saw us as a separate unit, which is really sad ... because I suppose, 'where's mummy and daddy?' 'Oh they've gone up to London with Kane'. 'Where's Mummy and Kane?' 'Oh they've gone to the clinic, oh they've gone there, oh they've gone there' and so the girls were just ... they haven't shown any resentment but they have had to tolerate ... what d'you call it ... I don't know whether it's dysfunctional or what, but it's certainly different ...

It is clear here that Neil's daughters are affected by their brother's presence in the family and that they notice the differences between their relationship with their parents and that of their brother. This example is not unusual when talking about the effects of the impaired child on the siblings.

For a quarter of my participants the effect on siblings was quite dramatic. Both Francis and Karen said that their daughter and son, respectively, became depressed for a period, and Tracy explained that all three of her other children (including David, the oldest with impairments) said they hated Brad, the youngest, and revealed that it had not only been emotionally traumatic but dangerous and frightening too.

> He's thrown knives at me; he's thrown knives at his brothers ... I was in tears all the time, erm ... his brothers were never happy, they hated him. ... He was in the bedroom with his brother because I told him to tidy up his bedroom ... and [his brother] was going, 'come on help' and Brad was about seven and he went ... and it was in a really deep voice, 'fucking cunt', and erm ... 'I'm going to chop you into pieces and flush you down the toilet'. And it was like ... and I stood there listening to this and it was like there was a man in the bedroom ... listening to that language and the way it was said, the animosity, and I went in there and Brad went, 'hi mum'. And it was almost like schizophrenic ... it was frightening ...

Tracy said that her son, 18 months older than Brad, began to wet the bed after his arrival, and added, 'I had no relationship with him [her non-impaired son], I wanted it, and craved it ... in a way it was like trying to keep everyone's life safe'.

These problems for the children concerned came about due to lack of time spent with the parent and the 'normal' sibling not being able to deal with the behaviour of the child with impairments. Francis told me that her daughter could not handle her brother.

> She spent most of her time in her bedroom; she couldn't handle any social situation with Mark at all. It just distressed her. She was just embarrassed ... she was very resentful to me and my husband for the time that we've had to give Mark.

Karen told me that her eldest son also suffered due to Kevin's problems.

> Kevin was very depressed, which was then making [my eldest son] depressed and it was all sort of going around ... he wasn't sleeping and he wasn't eating, but I was ... sort of connecting all of this together, until I went to the doctor.

Many of my participants who talked about the effects on their other children described situations such as not being able to go out with the impaired sibling or being unable to fully understand the difficulties.

Tina talked about how her relationship with her other two children had been different because of Teresa's impairments. Her daughters are twins, and Teresa had been identified with SPLD and dyspraxia. Tina's twin girls were unable to attend the nursery at the same time because the 'speech therapist told me ... that I was to have them go on separate sessions, so that I could spend as much time with Teresa at home ...' Added to this, her other daughter 'did think, "why has Teresa got all this and I haven't?"' At the nursery they both attended, Teresa had a learning support assistant, but her other daughter did not, and yet on the one day a week they attended nursery at the same time she told me that her other daughter would 'hang around the learning support assistant and go up to her as if to say look at what I've done ... to get her attention'.

As Teresa's difficulties became more apparent and the family began to spend large amounts of money on her specialist education and support, Tina told me that her oldest son was

> starting to be embarrassed by her, and he could see all the attention she was getting. ... He resented it and he knew we were spending

> money on her ... and I think he realised that it was the difference between going to Florida for a holiday and not. ... He was old enough to work out how much all of this was costing ...

Tina also said that Teresa 'used to come home everyday and scream for an hour ...' which had a negative effect on all of them, added to which her other daughter 'felt pushed out because she got the least attention', and her son felt resentful

> because he knew how much it would all cost and he wasn't get ... if he said, 'can I have a play station?' we'd say, 'no, we haven't got the money', and he was really resentful of that and all the time spent taking her to the child psychotherapist ...

Tina also revealed that her son accused her of double standards as illustrated here, '"You tell us off for doing what she does ..." and we have to have a different set of rules for her'. Clearly there is a lot of tension within this family household that affects both the parents and all of the children, as well as restricting them in their everyday life.

This research does not ask the siblings about their role within their family, and therefore these research findings are based upon the parents' interpretations of events. Even so, it is clear that given this and other research (Carpenter, 2000; Read, 2000; Seligman and Darling, 1997; Warren Dodd, 2004), an impaired child within the family can have a disabling effect. I see these effects as circular, that move from being internally, emotionally and locally driven, to feeding into both the political and cultural spheres via discourses on difference, difficulty, impairment and disability. In the next section I am going to document how the impaired child and the associated difficulties affect the main carers' life chances in relation to their working roles as mothers and carers.

## Professional parenting: the work involved

Working for a living in Britain is undeniably associated with being paid a wage, and yet a lot of work that is carried out is unpaid (Gittens, 1985). Work such as cooking, childcare, cleaning and caring for elderly, sick and impaired persons in an informal setting is often associated with unpaid labour, or work carried out in the name of duty or love. These are not new arguments as such, and it has been said that most of this type of 'care work' is predominantly female (Barnes et al., 1999; Morgan, 1996; Oakley, 1992; Ribbens, 1994; Smart and Neale, 1999). 'Care work' is not exclusively female though, and it has more recently been suggested that 'typical fathers can successfully transform themselves into typical mothers in terms of how they parent their children' (Smart and Neale, 1999: 107). Furthermore, as suggested by Bowring (2000), Levitas (1998, 2001) and Lister (1998), those who are unemployed or not in the paid labour market are more likely to experience social exclusion. Most of the parents in this research told me they do most, if not all, of the work associated with childrearing. Now for this group of parents the 'care work' also includes other types of work as indicated below. Later on in this section I will unpack the additional effects on mothers' or fathers' day-to-day lives. For example, some mothers have indicated their desire to work *outside* the home in paid employment as a form of respite or to simply 'escape'.

What is important here with regard to the family with an impaired child is how the impairment of the child affects the parents' lives in terms of their day-to-day labour, and how they negotiate the new and unexpected 'career' and what restrictions this 'career' may have on their life. I call the type of parenting that I am about to illustrate 'professional parenting' not because I believe there to be a type of training that can take place for the job, but because the mothers/fathers themselves take on different and additional roles, which require a more diverse range of skills than parenting in general. Furthermore, the level of gained independence of the impaired child (if any) may impact on whether or not the main carer follows their initial chosen career path (if they have one), substitutes it for an alternative one, does voluntary work or buys in additional help (nanny or au pair). Many of the mothers or fathers in this research have found themselves carrying out what I call extended early years support, based on extended personal care, as well as research and administration that goes beyond ordinary parenting. Furthermore, 'a direct consequence of having a disabled child is that the mother's participation in the paid labour market is severely constrained' (Barnes et al., 1999: 99–100).

Even a mother without an impaired child may take on 'quasi-professional characteristics. Such caring work may be increasingly informed by expertise and monitored by professionals even where these professionals do not take on a regular involvement in the business of caring' (Morgan, 1996: 99). The parents in this research not only have a high level of involvement with professionals, but over two-thirds (all three of the fathers are among these) made direct reference to their 'caring' role or 'work' that goes beyond the ordinary caring role of a mother or father. That is not to say those who did not make reference to this aspect of their childrearing process did not perform these roles. For example, Marlene, who has three sons, all with impairments, did make reference to restrictions on carrying out certain domestic work like 'the weekly shop'. She could not go shopping with her sons and therefore had to have respite funded by the local social services for two hours a week just so that she could get weekly shopping done, or simply have two hours *out of the house*.

Many of the parents found it necessary (if they were able) to study and research their child's impairment, and carry out such duties as advocacy, social work, administration, negotiation and mediation, physiotherapy, nursing and care work as part of their role, but others had additional paid work too. One-third of the participants were 'full time' mothers or fathers. And four out of the 24 parents worked full-time in paid employment: Neil (teacher), Francis (nurse), Kat (inclusion manager/qualified teacher) and Kim (fire-fighter). Half of the parents worked part-time in an array of occupations including accountancy, management consultancy, domestic cleaning, advocacy, care work, nursing, lecturing and bar work.

None of the parents said they resented any of the additional work or change of circumstances, but some of the parents did feel tired, sad, compromised, depressed and, at times, powerless in their parenting journey. Stella is one of the more positive participants (even though she did have a spell on anti-depressants) with regard to her family life. Her son's peers would have been more independent than him, but she told me,

> I think that when you have an able child they go to school, they do this, they go to university, and when you have a special needs child they go ... well who knows what they're going to do! [laughs] I mean it's a completely different path ... I will get something positive out of anything I do, whether it's a really bad situation ... and I've had a few challenges in my life that I never expected to have, and I'm determined to get something positive out of it and I think life's too short and you've got to make the most of it.

And yet she went on and said she still feels frustrated and restricted because

> if I mess that up [his routine] too much I could be in trouble elsewhere ... yes I'd love to do some more [study] but at this time it's not worth it. So I don't think it's the right thing to do. I keep trying to ... I'll apply for full-time jobs and talk myself into it ... it's ok, and then I don't get them and I'm relieved because I know I couldn't do them. And that's awful isn't it?... But people will say to me but you can't

compromise because you're a person as well. That is true, but you *do* have to compromise. I've had to compromise … you know courses … things that I want to do come second. They have to.

Stella has completed a diploma and advanced diploma in childcare and wants to be a social worker and yet is struggling to complete the course. For example, her son gets incredibly anxious if Stella is not at home after school, and the part-time course is an hour's drive away. It is clear that Stella does want to do something else other than care for her son and yet feels restricted and emotionally tied to her duty as a mother: love for her son, and indeed his health and welfare. Stella, with her complex desire to want to do 'something else' as well as care for her son, is not an unusual parent in this research.

Although 15 participants talked about their 'caring role', 10 spoke of how their impaired child affected their paid working life, and sometimes their sense of self. Francis did not actually want to stay at home with her son, and 'when all the childminding exhausted itself, and people wouldn't collect him after school and all that sort of thing … we [got] an au pair,' from the age of 3-1/2 until her son went to boarding school at the age of 11 years. Kerry spoke of the contradictions too, in her feelings about her work as a mother and what it involves with her sons, and revealed,

Why am I screaming for no reason? Why haven't I got any patience? You know all these questions, and all you want to do is love your children and bring them up best you can … but … the problems don't allow you to do that easily … I don't think it's a duty … it feels more than that … it's about having to fight…. When I'm doing all the work there's satisfaction out of that I'm doing the best for my children. I'm not saying it's not hard work because the letter writing takes time and because I'm dyslexic myself it takes me a day, if not more.

However, it is not only parents who have an impaired child who feel like they are not best equipped to mother.

Her worst fault as a mother was described as a lack of patience – "I haven't got a lot of patience and I should have …" Sandra found children more enjoyable as they got older, so that they become more independent with regard to the practicalities – "Once they can do for themselves, and they can sit and play a game properly, I've got far more patience then".

(Ribbens, 1994: 109)

This is crucial in thinking about mothering and caring for an impaired child. As parents in my research may never get to experience their children becoming independent adults which can intensify feelings of frustration in their loss; the journey of motherhood – birth to independence.

Una talked about her performance as a mother and how she felt about mothering and suggested that

> [you] actually have to perform as a parent ... when you have a child with a disability you have to perform as a parent ... you're not just allowed to be a parent, you have to perform. You have to be this icon of a perfect parent because you come into contact with so many professionals.

She resigned from her full-time position as a charity helpline manager and took up a part-time position when her research and administration skills were needed at home at one of the crucial transition stages in her son's life, and explained,

> I'm dropping out for the moment and taking a part-time role. It's so that I've got sufficient time to make myself very aware of the issues and legislation. You know, how many parents can afford to do that? I need at least two days a week free, I've got to go and research all the local colleges, and I've got to go and research all the specialist colleges, I've got to travel to do that. I've got to go to the housing associations and social services and I've got to get all the costing sorted out for all of this, nobody else is going to do it.

Una realised she was in a position to do that, having the educational qualifications and vocational experience to be able to get another job when her 'homework' or 'professional parenting' had been completed for that period. Furthermore, she had a supportive husband with economic security. In actual fact Una felt more able to do this type of work (research, administration and advocacy) than domestic care, and had she not had a child with impairments she would more than likely have remained in full-time paid employment. She stressed, 'don't get me wrong I love my children, but it doesn't necessarily make you an instinctive parent.... So the whole parenting thing has been a whole learning curve for me and I've learnt a hell of a lot ...'

Other parents in this research suggest that being a parent with an impaired child is like a full-time job, and they are therefore unable to return to a career, or maintain 'ordinary' mothering care work. As revealed by Tina and Trisha:

> Because I'm a chartered accountant I did envisage going back when they're five ... I did reorganise my career plans, and I had always intended to go back to work and I just said to my husband, 'I cannot do it'. She still has to go to occupational therapy, physiotherapy ... whatever, I still have to do programmes ... and I just could not do a full time job and keep taking times off to go to these things, and obviously you've got to do the OT [occupational therapy] stuff for half an hour when she gets home from school ... it's no good me coming home from work at seven o' clock exhausted and saying 'no I'm too tired to do it'. So I gave up on a full time career in accountancy.
>
> (Tina)

> I was very fortunate in the fact that I didn't work; because it was a full time job ... it was a full time job to find out everything and anything ... I mean anyone who does it and tries to work full time ... no way! Because of the phone calls, the reading, the contacts ...
>
> (Trisha)

All but one (Trisha) of the eight mothers who have talked about their full-time job as a mother suggested that they would not have continued being a full-time mother if they had been given the opportunity. None of the mothers blame the child for this compromise. And as Read (2000: 60) suggests in her research,

> [w]hatever the view of others, mothers tend not to characterise their disabled child as burdens to be shouldered. Studies consistently report mothers describing their disabled children with love, pride and appreciation.

However, even though parents may reflect upon their children fondly, Beresford still found that 'a third stated they would prefer to have a job. Aside of any financial gain, going to work can be a valuable source of support for a parent, providing an interest outside of the family' (1995: 14).

For some of the parents in my research gaining any kind of interest outside that of the family was not possible, and may not have been thought about. Jack had to give extended early years support and go to continuous hospital appointments, as well as negotiating with his son's mother (who had mental health problems). Tracy had to learn nursing skills for one of her sons, and had to provide continual support for Brad, while looking after her other two sons. She told me, 'it was years before he slept through the night'. These two parents and Marlene all had more than one child with impairments, were divorced or separated and lived on benefits. However, none of them described their work in the same way as those above. While Marlene did say that she wanted to 'better herself' by going back to college when the children were older, neither Tracy nor Jack gave any indication that they were compromised in their choices of 'potential' employment (even though they were both, at times, unhappy with their domestic situations). Tracy and Jack had limited or no qualifications, and so their life 'choices' even before their children were born were more limited than those mothers with a university education and assumed career paths.

It can be suggested here that these effects upon paid employment and the care work related to rearing an impaired child do have a disabling impact on the whole family. Even those mothers or fathers who 'chose' to and/or are financially secure enough to commit to full-time childrearing did not *necessarily* always feel satisfied with their mothering position. Moreover, half the participants worked in paid employment part-time, indicating the 'maternal part-time employment' trend since the 1960s in most advanced industrial societies (David et al., (1993: 33), but not necessarily for financial gain. However, parents of impaired children are often in an emotional and financial dilemma, as

> there has long been overwhelming evidence that bringing up a disabled child has a significant financial impact on the household. ... Simultaneously, however, the demands of caring reduce the options that parents, particularly mothers, have for gaining income by entering paid employment outside the home.
>
> (Read, 2000: 56)

All of the parents in this research have implied that their financial situation is worse than if they had not had an impaired child. However, some are in a better financial position than others: Stella is able to afford specialist residential boarding school because her husband works abroad much of the time to increase his income, Tina and her husband have spent thousands of pounds on specialist support and legal proceedings, and Trisha and her husband remortgaged their house with a view to paying for specialist education. It is clear that the child with impairments does have an effect on the family and indeed on what the mother/father does in relation to the 'care' work and beyond.

Although many women do carry out paid employment, albeit that may be part time, and some men do have responsibilities within the home, research suggests that a large majority of women are still prioritising childcare responsibilities (Morgan, 1996; Ribbens, 1994). However, if Beck and Beck-Gernsheim (1995: 106) are to be believed, an interesting notion as to why mothering or fathering a disabled child can be doubly difficult in late modern society is that

> [i]n highly industrialised societies people are trained to behave rationally, to be efficient, fast, disciplined and successful. A child represents the opposite, the 'natural' side of life, and that is exactly what is so appealing.

It is this 'promise' described so vividly that draws them to mothering. However, this 'natural' side of life is not really about getting back to nature, in the sense that the mothers and fathers expect animalistic and long-term dependency, but

> Being with a child will help them to rediscover some of their gifts and express some of their needs which they sorely miss in high-tech life: being patient, calm, solicitous and sensitive, affectionate, open and close. Motherhood seems to offer the women an alternative refuge from the working world, where it is imperative to behave responsibly and soberly, and emotions are generally considered a nuisance. Committing yourself to a child means contradicting the cognitive side of life, and finding a lifting counterweight to all that soul-destroying routine. As one woman remarks: "Where else can you find so much vital energy and joy as in a child?".
>
> (ibid.)

These above quotes seem a far cry from the feelings voiced by participants in this research. Given what was suggested in Chapter 3 with regard to expectations for their child and the mothering process, Beck and Beck-Gernsheim do seem to talk of a very different type of motherhood compared with the type described in this research, and not one that involved so much care and social work.

## Conclusions

This chapter ends the narrative-driven stories in highlighting the experiential aspect of the mothering journey within the social, political and cultural spheres described in the previous chapters. The chapter has suggested the following effects that can lead to the family being 'disabled'. The child with impairments affects the day-to-day living of the family by excluding them from outings and social gatherings. The mother or father was also isolated in a world where she or he had already compromised a large part of her or his potential working life, and felt unable to break free from it. This was experienced both personally and publicly as others' reactions to her or his impaired child resulted in a withdrawal from mainstream public places, and imposed exclusions from others.

The support networks are strained, and often the main carer of the child experiences a lack of support. The more impaired children in the family, the more likely the family will feel unsupported. The narratives suggested parents' mental health was dramatically affected by depression and anxiety, which were for some treated with anti-depressants and beta-blockers. Intense feelings of powerlessness and depression 'disabled' nearly half of my participants at some point in their life. This had an impact not only on the individual, but on the family as a whole. The main carer often has to maintain a longer period of responsibilities in the home. The role of the mother often changed into that of multi-functional professional parent, as social worker, advocate, carer and nurse, which then affected her potential career path. Furthermore, some parents chose to work outside the home, not only for financial gain, but also for respite. The career or work compromise was addressed and that conflicted with the extended the mothering role because the care of an impaired child often continues beyond that of her or his more able peers.

For most of the parents in this research the future seems bleak because they are unsure of what the future holds. Based on the lack of knowledge about certain impairments, their own mortality and the dependency levels of their children, the parents find it more difficult to focus on future projections. That, coupled with a view of the world that is split between 'our disabled world' and the 'real world', caused many to prefer to live one day/month/year at a time. However, most of the parents have bouts of depression and anxiety, and many have joined groups or made friends who support and empathise with their predicament. In many ways, it seems that *experienced relational support networks* are a key for mental stability, as is *feeling* and gaining support when support is expected. Support is expected not only within the private sphere among close social networks, but also in the cultural and political spheres, where, in a climate of high expectations, as inclusion is promoted and partnerships between professionals and parents promised.

# 7
# Discovering Difference, Experiencing Difficulty

## Introduction

> [...] exclusion is a gradient running from the credit rating of the
> well-off right down to the degree of dangerousness of the incarce-
> rated. Its currency is risk, its stance is *actuarial* – calculative and
> appraising. The image of society is not that of core insiders and a
> periphery of outsiders but more that of a beach where people are
> assigned to a gradient of positions in a littoral fashion. At the top of
> the beach there are the privileged sipping their cocktails, their place
> in the sun secured, while at the bottom there are creatures trapped
> in the sea who can only get out with great effort and even then are
> unlikely to survive. The beach has its gradient in between but this
> does not preclude at its extremes sharply segregated worlds,
> whether of the super-rich or the underclass [emphasis in original].
>
> (Young, 1999: 65)

As this quote suggests, the image of society is not a simple insiders or
outsiders dichotomy. Nor is it simply the case that sociology can gaze at
the public discourses on difficulty, difference, disappointment, denial
and exclusion and discover how such concepts are experienced personally
and privately without looking at the micro world of experience. The stark
reality for the parents in this study was not that they were sipping cock-
tails in a privileged position, nor were they trapped, unlikely to survive.
The participants in my research were 24 out of hundreds of thousands of
families who rear children with impairments. Moreover, when these
parents first discovered their baby or child had some kind of impairment, the expectations they unconsciously or consciously mapped did
not include difficult difference.

Cohen (2001), Craib (1994) and Young (1999) unpack what could seem like quite abstract notions of disappointment, denial, difficulty and exclusion. This book has drawn on their work, as well as on that of other sociologists who examine family structure and family practice both empirically and theoretically (for example, Beck and Beck-Gernsheim, 1995; Morgan, 1996; Ribbens, 1994 and Smart and Neale, 1999). Their work has shown how these abstract notions help to make sense of parents' personal narratives and my own biography in detailing the personal, emotional and social processes that are experienced privately, personally and publicly (Ribbens and Edwards, 1998; Ribbens McCarthy with Kirkpatrick, 2004 and Wright Mills, 1959).

Young (1999), as a critical criminologist, mapped a move from inclusion to exclusion during modernity through to late modernity. However, he points to the fact that the mode of exclusion is somewhat different in late modernity. It is one that shifts and is also dependent on one's 'credit rating' from the wealthy to the 'dangerousness of the incarcerated'. I would suggest that there is also a 'credit rating' for people who have impairments; only their credit is calculated within the frameworks of intelligence, mental ability, aesthetic beauty and appropriate social interaction. This 'credit rating' affects parents of the impaired child, the child and the extended family, and is therefore calculated on a continuum of 'normal' family practices. This renders the family 'disabled', difficult and excluded, with a very low 'credit rating' in terms of worth regarding inclusion into mainstream society.

Cultural assumptions and directives that are imposed upon the personal and emotional process place a burden on the expectations of childrearing. For example, notions of childrearing practices are uncovered in 'mother craft' manuals (Spock, 1946/1973; Stoppard, 1984) and in psychology literature (Winnicot, 1964), and explicitly illustrate what mothers should and should not be feeling and how to rear a healthy child. It has been found that for many parents their parenting journey began with coping or dealing with the emotional 'loss' of a child that was imagined. Cultural assumptions about the grotesque, imperfect and mentally impaired were introduced initially in Chapter 2, and then expanded upon throughout the book. These assumptions are psychologically deep-seated unlike those imposed upon parents in the childrearing handbooks and social policy directives. Not only do the parents themselves have to deal with these assumptions, but also, they are all too often explicitly present in the reactions of others.

Issues regarding an individual's 'credit rating', emotional responses and family practices need to be understood in relation to both the private and personal world and the public social world, that is to say, within and between the social, cultural and political spheres. Neither can be fully understood without the other. I refer back to Wright Mills, who suggested in *The Sociological Imagination* that neither 'the life of an individual nor the history of society can be understood without understanding both' (1959: 3), the private and public worlds. He goes on to suggest that individuals, though, do not necessarily relate their individual circumstances to such history (ibid.). In this research my participants talk openly about their private and intimate thoughts about parenting their impaired child. It has been my aim to bring together these personal narratives in analysing public discourses on difference and difficulty, denial and disappointment, and exclusion and inclusion. Although a small-scale study, my participants are a sample of parents who rear children with impairments. The sociological significance of this research rests not only on the intimate in-depth narratives that unfold, but also on the scale of the population with similar problems: there are at least a quarter of a million children who have a statement of SEN in England and Wales (DfES, 2004a). The families and their social networks, support groups, and the health, social and education services are all affected by the issues highlighted in this empirical research, emphasising the contemporary significance of this topic and the need for further research.

The key themes that run through this book are that of disappointment, denial and social exclusion and inclusion. All three are experienced at different levels both emotionally and practically. These emotional and practical difficulties affect the mental health, social relationships, career prospects and general everyday living conditions for parents of children with impairments. However, an equally important issue is also apparent in the analysis of policy documents and cultural discourses. Denial of difficulty is found in policies on inclusive education where inclusion is in name only, and in how the public responds to difficulty in their aversion to difficult difference and the difficult other.

Ultimately what this book does is demonstrate that mothering a child with impairments is difficult. Parents find themselves disappointed, excluded, isolated, compromised and frustrated. However, in the face of this I revealed that even though parents have been depressed, taken anti-depressants, turned to alcohol, felt suicidal, suffered in their relationships or wanted to desert their children, many have fought the health and education system, shown resilience, set up self-help groups, complained and, most importantly, demonstrated that their children with all their impairments were worth fighting for. I would now like to turn to the social, cultural and political spheres and key concepts in more detail.

# Within the social, cultural and political spheres

## The social, cultural and political spheres

In thinking sociologically about how disappointment, denial and exclusion can be viewed and responded to more broadly, and how they can be discussed as tools in analysing other difficult differences, I suggest looking at the social, cultural and political spheres. The political and cultural spheres permeate and, to a certain extent, circulate around, the social sphere, like planets circulating and impacting upon the Earth. The social sphere includes the internal emotional experiences of (in this case) mothering an impaired child, combined with her external relations within her personal world (relationships with family and friends, for example) and her public world (relationships with professional others and public others, for example).

Both the cultural and political spheres impact upon the social sphere in every way, and both are historically specific. In the case of this research the cultural sphere includes deep psychic aversions to difficult difference such as public displays of socially inappropriate behaviour and the 'uncivilised'. The political sphere includes political discourses on inclusion and policy documents and directives on inclusive education. In mothering an impaired child it seems that the cultural and political spheres impact negatively, in the main, but it is feasible to think that changes within the cultural and political spheres could dramatically impact positively on the social sphere, and therefore on individuals and groups within society. For this research I looked at disappointment, denial, inclusion and exclusion. These concepts have been analysed within all spheres. For example, denial is analysed both socially as an emotional response to discovering difference *and* politically as inclusive education policies compete and conflict with other political discourses on academic excellence and examination cultures.

### Disappointment

This research has shown some of the ways in which parenting an impaired child is punctuated with experiences of disappointment: from disappointment of the identification of an impairment to disappointment in the education system, in health and local authority professionals and in social relations both inside and outside the family. In Chapter 3, Kim was disappointed because she felt cheated out of the celebration of birth, and Kerry because not only did her first son have impairments, so did her second. Lynne felt disappointed because her son was assessed as having a low IQ. These types of disappointments tap into preconceived expectations, not experienced and explicit unless there is an omission of what was expected: for example, lack of celebration at birth, a child's lack of intellectual ability or a lack of socially appropriate behaviour.

Disappointment is also experienced in relation to the official systems in place for the education of an impaired child. For example, in Chapter 4, Jack was initially disappointed that his son was eventually placed in a school for children with severe learning impairments having initially tried mainstream school and a school for children with moderate learning impairments. Francis was disappointed because her family was initially blamed for the anti-social behaviour of her son. The majority of participants in my research were disappointed in general with the system because they came into conflict with education professionals when their expectations were steeped in assumptions about a 'partnership' with professionals.

Expectations also led to a loss, and therefore disappointment for the self too. In Chapter 6, Stella consistently suggested that she wanted a career outside the home by going for job interviews and retraining, and yet she felt unable to pursue these desires fully because of her additional commitments to her impaired son. Disappointment for the self too was highlighted by many of my participants in their expectations of support. Emotional and practical support was not always forthcoming from close relations, friendship networks or official institutions such as the social services, as detailed in Chapters 4–6.

For Craib, disappointment is a crucial part of personal human growth and development in late modern society. Too many individuals shy away from relationships and social situations that become difficult, to the point of disappointment. Craib points out that

> [i]f I put a hand in the fire and it is burnt, I will not do it again in a hurry; psychotherapy says, in one sense, put your hand in the fire and keep it there. Psychological development depends on 'staying' in the fire, to the point where we begin to understand the pain and find that it is bearable, and that it might even be used in some way. This is a process which perhaps other ages might simply have called 'life', and it certainly has to do with being, not with doing.
>
> (1994: 193)

Because parents in this study do not want to, or simply cannot shy away from their children they have to face these disappointments. Babs had a two-year separation from her husband as a result of difficulties and disappointments with her life and her relationship. They dealt with and lived with all of these difficulties, and she and her husband reunited, with a stronger bond.

What this research finds is that rearing a child with an impairment, and more specifically, one that affects his or her educational achievement is disappointing and difficult to accept, but parents do – even though others may find it difficult, showing little more than pity or even anger towards these parents. For some parents the difficulty was in convincing health or education professionals that there was an impairment or need, compounded by the fact that the parents were often unsure of what the problem actually was. All of the parents stressed the importance of professional recognition of the impairment and indeed a label for it. It was the label of the impairment that often triggered support from the professionals, especially within education. For my participants a label was also a tool that enabled them to move forward both practically and emotionally, rendering them no longer helpless but very much involved in the process and therefore alleviating some of the disappointment.

*Denial*

Difficulties that parents experienced in this study began with coping or dealing with the emotional loss of a child that was imagined or dreamed of. The birth or early months, for parents whose child's impairment was identified at birth or very early on, were marred and the expected celebration never took place. Some parents, for a short time, *denied* that there was an impairment even though it had been explicitly identified. In relation to heart and cancer patients, Cohen (2001) suggests that there are different types of denial, but in the main the patient fluctuates between an awareness of the condition, or total denial. He argues that different types of denial can affect the actual life chances of the patient, and that 'realistic' passive acceptance, in a longitudinal study with cancer patients, decreased their survival chances, whereas fighting or living with an optimistic belief, or complete denial increased their chances of survival. In the case of parents, I would suggest their mental health is improved with optimistic fighting strategies or denial of the severity of impairment as highlighted in Chapter 6. 'Mental health, it turns out, depends not on being in touch with reality, but on illusion, self-deception and denial' (ibid.: 56).

For most parents once the impairment had been named, or identified, the process of coming to terms with it began, but as suggested, they moved in and out of acceptance and denial. Even though some parents indicated that they did not want this difficulty, none of them gave up. The narratives revealed the process was more about realising the difficulty, and then moving on, in the hope that others such as health and education professionals, as well as family members and the public others would do the same with acceptance and support. Parents, understandably (even if for a short time), do not want to recognise that their child has an impairment. When they do, as detailed in Chapter 5, imply there are *hierarchies of impairments*. As a form of denial Kerry consistently referred to her oldest son as 'only' having a speech and language difficulty *not* a learning disability. Others suggested that their child was 'not that bad' always using a more impaired child as an (ab)normalising barometer.

Parents' experiences of denial also include that of professional denial, which could also be discussed in relation to this 'barometer'. A shortage of public funding and specialists within LEA and social services for assessments and specialist provision and support means that professionals are manoeuvred into concentrating their energies on more severe cases. Although how 'severe' is interpreted is questionable. Recall Tracy and Marlene, in Chapter 5, who both asked for help in times of crisis and both were denied the help they needed.

As with disappointment, the data, literature and documents in this study not only suggest that denial occurs within the social sphere (at a personal, emotional and private level) but that it also occurs within the cultural and political spheres. As suggested here, denial is present within social inclusion and inclusive education policy discourses. In the promotion of inclusive education, an attempt to combine all difficult differences and therefore deny or normalise aspects of impairment is apparent. I refer to the changes in labelling impairments from imbecile, maladjusted and educationally subnormal, to children with 'special educational needs'. Alongside this was a move towards including, 'where possible' such children in mainstream schools. This can have a normalising effect, but to normalise is to deny the severity of difficulty. Cohen would call this macro-denial and suggests, 'Denial and normalization reflect personal and cultural states in which suffering is not acknowledged' (2001: 52). While inclusive mainstream education is promoted as the first option over and above specialist provision the latter will seem second best and therefore is assumed as second rate (as detailed in Chapter 5), which refers the reader back to the opening quote in relation to 'credit ratings' and worth. This takes us to issues of exclusion.

*Exclusion*

In this research, debates and discourses around inclusion or exclusion, integration or segregation and insider or outsider, on children identified with SEN, and wider sociological debates are crucial. However, while I agree that it is a human right for families not to be excluded and marginalised within society I do not find the 'human rights equals inclusive education' (Armstrong and Barton, 1999) debate on disability to be helpful when discussing the actual *education* of children with impairments.

There are many arguments about who should and who should not be included, integrated or experience life as an 'insider' both at a political macro level (Oliver, 1996; Shakespeare, 1994) and at a micro and policy level (Armstrong et al., 2000; Vincent, 2000). In the opening of this chapter I referred to Young's (1999) use of 'credit ratings' and 'worth' in relation to this study. It is clear to me that there are significant similarities between theoretical and empirical research on deviance and criminality and research on impairment and disability. Both deal with issues of difference, difficulty, stigma, public perception and exclusion. For the participants in my research, exclusion and isolation were experienced throughout their lives with reference to their own experience and their experience felt via their child's exclusion.

Parents in this study have excluded themselves from going into certain social situations because of their fear of others' reactions, their fear for their child's safety and for those around them. As detailed in Chapter 3, Kerry was horrified when her son injured another child and that child's mother verbally abused her in front of 30 other mothers. This type of reaction, in addition to her son's behaviour, made her think twice about the places she visited. Neil too said that he and his family became isolated because of his son's lack of fear and high-pain threshold. The fear of risk and harm was referred to by many of my participants, especially those who had children identified with AD/HD or who were on the autistic spectrum. Exclusion from the paid work force is also evident in this research, as parents became 'professional parents'.

With regard to crime, difference and difficulty, Young commented that '[t]he late modern world is both ingesting and ejecting, it absorbs diversity and it provides a gradient of tolerance which is both including and excluding' (1999: 65). I have found similarities in this study as exclusion is also found within inclusive education practices and discourses. Inclusive education suggests tolerance of difference with regard to low educational achievement and yet high standards in academic achievement are privileged over and above non-academic achievements through systems of inter- and intraschool competition.

Moving this discussion into the field of social policy, these statements above transcend the social, cultural and political spheres. The causes of tensions are around inclusive education regarding both the children and the testing and examination culture. As with Young's description of the late modern world being including and excluding, I suggest here that mainstream education, in name, includes many impaired children but in practice excludes them at different levels, practically, intellectually and emotionally. By looking beyond disability and impairment I would expect to be able to think about these three concepts more broadly and develop further research around the social, cultural and political spheres and their relationships within and between each other theoretically and empirically.

## Problematic inclusive discourses and the 'disabled' family

Contradictions that arise from education policy and provision, and from the discourses of inclusion, often result in parents having difficulty in negotiating the 'official' education process, or constantly 'fight the system'. Studies have shown that parents have been drawn into the debate; public policy has accentuated tensions between individual rights and interests and collective justice and equity (Norwich, 2000 and Simmons, 2000). This has caused a divide among common interest groups (parents of children with SEN): those who want children to be included in mainstream education, to 'fit in' to society and those who believe that inclusive education only exacerbates the problems the child faces socially and educationally. I illustrate that although important, these debates are divisive.

These discourses are not about inclusion or exclusion but about negotiating an appropriate education for *all* children. If fully inclusive education and discourses on acceptance and celebration of difference are to be successful, then engagement with the social, cultural and political spheres, in this case, for families of children with SEN then the following manifesto must be debated.

- An original discourse on '(em)bodied difference' is considered, and acceptance and celebration of difference should be in someway integrated, rather than the discourse on 'tolerance' that seems to be seeping into cultural attitudes. This feeds into debates and discourses around 'inclusion'/exclusion of children identified with SEN and their families and wider sociological debates about 'difference' and difficulty.
- Develop a holistic notion of social inclusion and inclusive education, eradicate ignorance of special education and promote local different education sites. This will deliver a whole education approach not necessarily focusing on the mainstream as being 'inclusive' and will

promote a social 'local' community. If different provision is made, this provision ought not to be seen as exclusionary but as a means of promoting a wider notion of inclusion within adult life and society.

* A partnership between schools and parents, indicated above, is a reality not rhetorical. A language and advocacy system that supports *all* parents and carers of children with SEN and not simply those who shout the loudest. (Significantly, 'shouting loudest' may be an important point. In 2002–3 there were 91,430 admission appeals lodged by parents, 63,960 were heard by an appeals committee and 21,360 were found in favour of the parents (DfES, 2004a) indicating that over three quarters of the parents went though this official process and lost their appeal).

Within the political sphere policies directed towards provision and its implementation of special education directly affect the social sphere and therefore families and their impaired children. Moreover, these children have a right to be educated in a way that is best suited to the individual. Therefore education is not simply a need but a right to have the most appropriate education. The contradictions that occur between the theories and policies imply the experience within the social sphere dramatically affects the emotional and practical lives of the families involved. This is based on the heterogeneity of provision at the local level and wider society reactions to difference and disability. The privileging of the academic and the 'normal' can exclude the child with SEN and their families from engaging in a so-called inclusive society. Therefore parents and the educational professionals continue to struggle with inclusion versus academic excellence.

In 'disabling' a family the notion of disability could be paralleled with experiences related to physical impairment, here in this research, with stories of exclusion, stigmatisation, isolation, prejudice and pain (Morris, 1991; Slack, 1999). In thinking about the family and the social sphere it could be argued there are two levels of experience and disability. At macro level, the cultural sphere suggests disabilism is imposed upon the family or individual based on their disability; and at a micro level, as experiences and emotional responses impact upon the disabled person or member of their family. In thinking about disability, I like Sandy Slack's use of the Alice in Wonderland quoted here:

I wonder if I've been changed in the night? Let me think: was I the same when I got up this morning? I almost think I can remember feeling a little different. But if I'm not the same, the next question is, 'Who in the world am I?' Ah, that's the great puzzle.

(in Slack, 1999: 28)

Slack says that had she not been disabled, 'I would have missed out on meeting some amazing people committed to ensuring rights for disabled people. I would certainly be more financially secure but would I be any happier?' (Slack, 1999: 30). Morris (1991) too *became* disabled and mirrors this. That said, neither is suggesting that becoming disabled has been easy and a preferred life path. But they have turned experiences around to ensure that most benefit from their lives, and the lives of others with impairments as proactively as possible. The families described in this study too have *become* 'disabled'. The child with the impairments may have been born with them, but the family had to adjust emotionally and practically to the impairments and the disability discourses that confront them. For many of the parents in this research, frustrations and emotional anxiety as well as depression are a result of being unable to carry out 'ordinary' daily tasks, such as shopping.

It is clear from my research and that of others, such as Oakley (1992), any kind of social support is crucial in childrearing, both generally and particularly, for those families with impaired children. In addition to this support she or he may yearn to (or does in fact) work outside the home as a form of respite rather than simply because the money is necessary. Parents are often too tired emotionally and practically to fight for the family as a whole (for example, their relationships with other family members), based on their difficulties with their impaired child or children who have what seems like more urgent needs both educationally, socially and sometimes medically. Therefore the family and familial relationships can suffer at the hands of a child's impairments where social policy and public support could in fact ease the process for parents and their family.

## ... Finally

In tying together the themes in this book I turn to Wright Mills (1959) and Sibley (1995) in an attempt to highlight the significance of the broader sociological issues within a spatial frame. Wright Mills (1959: 8) explains that by using history and biography via the 'sociological imagination' the social researcher can tap into personal troubles of the individual and public issues of society. For example, he considers marriage, war and unemployment, all of which have both personal and emotional considerations, but also have a massive impact on the social, economic and political fabric of society. Within this book I have considered the personal impacts of mothering, impairment, disability, education policy, health and education institutions and the family. Moreover, these issues are of public concern and have been discussed and unpacked according to personal history, biography and policy.

I find the geographer Sibley (1995) useful in his discussion about borders and boundaries. The work here finds the relationship between the personal/private and public/other troubling and yet this does not mean that it is always unnecessary or something to be avoided (recall Ian Craib's work too). Sibley (1995: 33) discusses '[z]ones of ambiguity in spatial and social categorizations' between the private and public, and adult and child. He claims that at the crossover there is a grey area, a liminal zone that is a 'source of anxiety' and should be eliminated (ibid.). Sibley suggests that individuals, though, are unable to organise themselves into clear-cut divisions. I propose that it may not be fruitful or desirable to have these divisions, as in the case of research methodology, constructions of difference, the private and the public, dependency and independency and 'inclusive' education. In dealing with these dilemmas, parents, professionals, policymakers and the public others need to address such issues as:

- The adult and child in relation to how dependency and independency are perceived: not all impaired children will ever become independent, gain full employment and enter the mainstream environment. This does not make them any less human.
- Impairment or non-impairment and (dis)ability or ability. There are clearly categories of impairment that are *actual*, regardless of what label is placed upon the difficulty. For example, a child with intellectual impairments and SPLD will be challenging for the main carer. However, social policy directives and public responses can ease the process.

But is it actually about easing the process? If we are to consider Ian Craib's work on disappointment then it is not so much about easing the process but limiting expectation. If expectation about the 'perfect', or even normal, or the fantasy about cleanliness and order were eradicated then mothering a child with impairment would not seem so difficult. (But not to deny the *actual* day-to-day difficulties are still there). And yet it seems that disgust and aversion to difficult difference goes back further than the arrival of an individualistic consumer society obsessed with the perfect body, mind and spirit. Coming to terms with disability and particularly intellectual impairment is entrenched in the psyche of our past times as well as in the 21st century (recall Swift's [1967 {1726}] work on his aversion to the 'impure' and 'uncivilised' and not least of all the 'eugenics programme' in modern and indeed post modern times).

The conversations in the interviews were specifically about discovering difference and experiencing the education process, especially identification, assessment and statementing. This book contributes not only to the literature on parenting an impaired child, disability, special education and qualitative methodology, but more broadly it seeks to understand some of the deep-seated cultural assumptions about difference and difficulty, alongside 'new' assumptions and directives, imposed upon the individual and families. Political and theoretical constructions of difference and disability via categories and classifications, alongside historical constructions and concepts of difference based on educational and social 'abnormalities', are the main theoretical threads drawing on disappointment, denial and exclusion. Out of this a tolerance of difference was apparent. To tolerate difference is to 'put up with' rather than accept. To accept difference is not to accept failure and underachievement but to accept the idiosyncratic aspects of the human being within this social context.

Politically, the national expectation of educational ability has become more competitive. Privileging academic qualifications with inter- and intraschool competition means children with SEN are at best 'tolerated' and at worst singled out for abuse or exclusion. The contradictions that occur between the theories and policies imply that the experience at a local level dramatically affects the emotional and practical lives of the families involved. This is based on the heterogeneity of provision at the local level and wider social reactions to difference and disability. The privileging of the academic and the 'normal' can exclude the child with SEN and their families from engaging in a so-called inclusive society. I have examined ideas about disappointment, denial and exclusion and proposed that differences and difficulties should be accepted not as imperfect and less than human but as *all too human.*

# Bibliography

Adler, P. and Adler, P. (1997) 'Parent-as-researcher: the politics of researching in the personal life' in Hertz, R. (ed.) *Reflexivity and Voice* London: Sage Publications, pp. 21–44.

Allan, J. (1999) *Actively Seeking Inclusion* London: Falmer Press.

Armstrong, F., Armstrong, D. and Barton, L. (2000) (eds) *Inclusive Education: Policy, Contexts and Comparative Perspectives* London: David Fulton Publishers.

Armstrong, F. and Barton, L. (1999) (eds) *Disability, Human Rights and Education: Cross-Cultural Perspectives* Buckingham: Open University Press.

Audit Commission (2002) *Special Educational Needs: A Mainstream Issue* London: Audit Commission.

Avery, D. M. (1999) 'Talking "tragedy": identity issues in the parental story of disability' in Corker, M. and French, S. (eds) (1999) *Disability Discourse* Buckingham: Open University, pp. 116–26.

Baldwin, S. and Carlisle, J. (1999) 'Living with disability: the experiences of parents and children' in Allen, G. (ed.) *The Sociology of the Family* Oxford: Blackwell Publishers, pp. 340–63.

Barnes, C., Mercer, G. and Shakespeare, T. (1999) *Exploring Disability: A Sociological Introduction* Cambridge: Polity Press.

Beck, U. and Beck-Gernsheim, E. (1995) *The Normal Chaos of Love* Cambridge: Polity Press.

Becker, H. (1963/1973) *Outsiders: Studies in the Sociology of Deviance* New York: The Free Press.

Benjamin, S. (2002) *The Micropolitics of Inclusive Education: An Ethnography* Buckingham: Open University Press.

Benn, M. (1998) *Madonna and Child: Towards a New Politics of Motherhood* London: Jonathan Cape.

Beresford, B. (1995) *Expert Opinions: A National Survey of Parents Caring for a Severely Disabled Child* Bristol: Policy Press in association with the Joseph Rowntree Foundation and Community Care.

Bowring, F. (2000) 'Social exclusion: limitations of the debate' *Critical Social Policy* 20 (3), pp. 307–30.

Braun, D. (2001) 'Perspectives on parenting' in Foley, P., Roche, J. and Tucker, S. (eds) *Children in Society: Contemporary Theory, Policy and Practice* Basingstoke: Palgrave, pp. 239–48.

Carpenter, B. (2000) 'Sustaining the family: meeting the needs of families of children with disabilities' *British Journal of Special Education* 27 (3), pp. 135–44.

Chadwick, R. (1987) 'The perfect baby: introduction' in Chadwick, R. (ed.) *Ethics, Reproduction and Genetic Control* London: Routledge, pp. 93–135.

Clarke, J. and Glendinning, C. (2002) 'Partnership and the remaking of welfare governance' in Glendinning, C., Powell, M. and Rummery, K. (eds) *Partnerships, New Labour and the Governance of Welfare* Bristol: The Policy Press, pp. 33–50.

Cohen, S. (2001) *States of Denial: Knowing about Atrocities and Suffering* Cambridge: Polity Press.

Cole, B. (2004) *Mothers-Teachers: Insights into Inclusion* London: David Fulton Publishers.

Coward, R. (1997) 'The heaven and hell of mothering: mothering and ambivalence in the mass media' in Hollway, W. and Featherstone, B. (eds) *Mothering and Ambivalence* London: Routledge, pp. 111–18.

Craib, I. (1994) *The Importance of Disappointment* London: Routledge.

Crozier, G. and Reay, D. (2004) (eds) *Activating Participation: Parents and Teachers Working Towards Partnership* Stoke on Trent: Trentham Books.

Culpitt, I. (1999) *Social Policy and Risk* London: Sage Publications.

Darlington, C. (2004) 'We are still challenged by the concept of difference' *The Independent* 10 June.

David, M., Edwards, R., Hughes, M. and Ribbens, J. (1993) *Mothers and Education: Inside Out? Exploring Family-Education Policy and Experience* London: Macmillan.

DES (1978) *Special Educational Needs Report of the Committee of Enquiry in the Education of Children and Young People* London: Department of Education and Science.

DfEE (1993) *Education Act* London: Department of Education and Employment.

DfEE (1996) *Education Act* London: Department for Education and Employment.

DfEE (1997a) *Excellence For All Children: Green Paper* London: Department for Education and Employment.

DfEE (1997b) *Excellence in Schools: White Paper* London: Department for Education and Employment.

DfES (2001a) *Code of Practice on the Identification and Assessment of Special Educational Needs* London: Department for Education and Skills.

DfES (2001b) *Special Educational Needs and Disability Act* London: Department for Education and Skills.

DfES (2003) *Statistics of Education: Schools in England: January 2003* London: Department for Education and Skills.

DfES (2004a) *Statistics of Education: Schools in England: January 2003* London: Department for Education and Skills.

DfES (2004b) *Pupils Characteristics and Class Sizes in Maintained Schools in England: January 2004* London: Department for Education and Skills.

DfES (2004c) *Special Educational Needs in England: January 2004* London: Department of Education and Skills.

Docking, J. (2000) 'What is the solution? an overview of national policies for schools, 1979–99' in Docking, J. (ed.) *New Labour's Policies for Schools Raising the Standard?* London: David Fulton Publishers, pp. 21–42.

Donzelot, J. (1979) *The Policing of Families* London: Johns Hopkins University Press.

Douglas, J. W. B. (1964) *The Home and the School* Herts: Panther Books Ltd.

Douglas, M. (1966) *Purity and Danger* London: Routledge.

Edwards, R. and Mauthner, M. (2002) 'Ethics and feminist research: theory and practice' in Mauthner, M., Birch, M., Jessop, J. and Miller, T. (eds) *Ethics in Qualitative Research* London: Sage Publications, pp. 14–31.

Emerson, E. (2003) 'Mothers of children and adolescents with intellectual disability: social and economic situation, mental health status, and the self-assessed social and psychological impact of the child's difficulties' *Journal of Intellectual Disability Research* 47 (4/5), pp. 385–99.

Forna, A. (1998) *Mother of All Myths: How Society Moulds and Constrains Mothers* London: HarperCollins Publishers.

Foucault, M. (1973) *The Birth of the Clinic* London: Tavistock.

Foucault, M (1976) *The History of Sexuality* Harmondsworth: Penguin.
Foucault, M. (1977) *Discipline and Punish: The Birth of the Prison* London: Tavistock.
Foucault, M. (1980) *Power/Knowledge* Hertfordshire: Harvester Wheatsheaf.
Friel, J. (1997) *Children with Special Needs: Caught in the Acts* London: Jessica Kingsley Publishers Ltd.
Furedi, F. (2001) *Paranoid Parenting: Abandon Your Anxieties and Be a Good Parent* Harmondsworth: Penguin Books Ltd.
Gascoigne, E. (1995) *Working with Parents as Partners in SEN* London: David Fulton Publishers.
Gillies, V. and Alldred, P. (2002) 'The ethics of intention: research as a political tool' in Mauthner, M., Birch, M., Jessop, J. and Miller, T. (eds) *Ethics in Qualitative Research* London: Sage Publications, pp. 32–52.
Gittens, D. (1985) *The Family in Question: Changing Households & Familiar Ideologies* Basingstoke: Macmillan.
Glendinning, C., Powell M. and Rummery, K. (2002) *Partnerships, New Labour and the Governance of Welfare* Bristol: The Policy Press.
Goffman, E. (1963) *Stigma: Notes on the Management of Spoiled Identity* Harmondsworth: Penguin Books.
Goffman, E. (1969) *The Presentation of Self in Everyday Life* Harmondsworth: Penguin Books.
Gray, D. E. (2002) '"Everybody just freezes. Everybody is just embarrassed": felt and enacted stigma among parents of children with high functioning autism' *Sociology of Health and Illness* 24 (6), pp. 734–49.
Hilpern, K. (2004) 'Unlocking everyone's potential' *The Independent* 10 June.
Hollway, W. and Featherstone, B. (1997) (eds) *Mothering and Ambivalence* London: Routledge.
Levitas, R. (1998) *The Inclusive Society? Social Exclusion and New Labour* Basingstoke: Macmillan.
Levitas, R. (2001) 'Against work: a utopian incursion into social policy' *Critical Social Policy* 21 (4), pp. 449–65.
Liddiard, M. (1954) *The Mothercraft Manual* 12th edn London: Churchill.
Lindsay, G. (2003) 'Inclusive education: a critical perspective' *British Journal of Special Education* 30 (1), pp. 3–12.
Lister, R. (1998) 'From equality to social inclusion: New Labour and the welfare state' *Critical Social Policy* 18 (54–7).
Maclure, S. (1992) *Education Re-formed* London: Hodder & Stoughton.
Mactavish, J. B. and Schleien, S. J. (2004) 'Re-injecting spontaneity and balance in family life: parents' perspectives on recreation in families that include children with developmental disability' *Journal of Intellectual Disability Research* 48 (2) 1, pp. 23–141.
Maes, B., Broekman, T.G., Dosen, A. and Nauts, J. (2003) 'Caregiving burden of families looking after persons with intellectual disability and behavioural or psychiatric problems' *Journal of Intellectual Disability Research* 47 (6), pp. 447–55.
McDonnell, P. (2000) 'Inclusive education in Ireland: rhetoric and reality' in Armstrong, F., Armstrong, D. and Barton, L. (eds) *Inclusive Education: Policy, Contexts and Comparative Perspectives* London: David Fulton Publishers Ltd, pp. 12–26.
Miller, O. (2000) 'Inclusion and the voluntary sector' in Daniels, H. (ed.) *Special Education Reformed: Beyond Rhetoric* London: Falmer Press, pp. 241–54.

Miller, T. (2005) *Making Sense of Motherhood: A Narrative Approach* Cambridge: Cambridge University Press.

Moore, H. L. (1996) 'Mothering and social responsibilities in a cross-cultural perspective' in Bortolaia Silva, E. (ed.) *Good Enough Mothering: Feminist Perspectives On Lone Motherhood* London: Routledge, pp. 58–75.

Morgan, D. H. J. (1996) *Family Connections: An Introduction to Family Studies* Cambridge: Polity Press.

Morris, J. (1991) *Pride Against Prejudice: Transforming Attitudes to Disability* London: The Women's Press Ltd.

Morris, J., Abbot, D. and Ward, L. (2003) 'Disabled children and residential schools: the implications for local education professionals' *British Journal of Special Education* 30 (2), pp. 70–5.

Norwich, B. (2000) 'Inclusion in education' in Daniels, H. (ed.) *Special Education Reformed: Beyond Rhetoric?* London: Falmer Press, pp. 5–30.

Oakley, A. (1981a) *From Here to Maternity: Becoming a Mother,* Harmondsworth: Pelican Books.

Oakley, A. (1981b) 'Interviewing women' in Roberts, H. (ed.) *Doing Feminist Research* London: Routledge & Kegan Paul Ltd, pp. 30–61.

Oakley, A. (1992) *Social Support and Motherhood* Oxford: Blackwell Publishers.

Observer Magazine (2003) 'Standing up for Down's'. 1 June.

Oliver, M. (1996) *Understanding Disability: From Theory to Practice* Basingstoke: Macmillan.

Parker, R. (1997) 'The production and purposes of maternal ambivalence' in Hollway, W. and Featherstone, B. (eds) *Mothering and Ambivalence* London: Routledge, pp. 17–36.

Phillipson, C., Allan, G. and Morgan, D. (2004) (eds) *Social Networks and Social Exclusion: Sociological and Policy Perspectives* Hants: Ashgate.

Plummer, K. (1995) *Telling Sexual Stories: Power, Change and Social Worlds* London: Routledge.

Read, J. (2000) *Disability, the Family and Society: Listening to Mothers* Buckingham: Open University Press.

Reay, D. (1998) *Class Work: Mothers' Involvement in Their Children's Primary Schooling* London: UCL Press.

Ribbens, J. (1994) *Mothers and Their Children: A Feminist Sociology of Childrearing* London: Sage Publications.

Ribbens, J. (1998) 'Hearing my feeling voice? An autobiographical discussion of motherhood' in Ribbens, J. and Edwards, R. (eds) *Feminist Dilemmas in Qualitative Research: Public Knowledge and Private Lives* London: Sage Publications, pp. 24–38.

Ribbens, J. and Edwards, R. (1998) (eds) *Feminist Dilemmas in Qualitative Research: Public Knowledge and Private Lives* London: Sage Publications.

Ribbens McCarthy, J. with Kirkpatrick, S. (2004) 'Negotiating public and private: maternal mediations or home-school boundaries' in Crozier, G. and Reay, D. (eds) *Activating Participation: Parents and Teachers Working Towards Partnership* Stoke on Trent: Trentham Books.

Richardson, D. (1993) *Women, Motherhood and Childrearing* London: The Macmillan Press Ltd.

Riddell, S. (2000) 'Inclusion and choice: mutually exclusive principles in special educational needs?' in Armstrong, F., Armstrong, D. and Barton, L. (eds) *Inclusive Education: Policy, Contexts and Comparative Perspectives* London: David Fulton Publishers Ltd, pp. 99–116.

Rioux, M. (1999) 'Inclusive education in Canada: a piece in the equality puzzle' in Armstrong, F. and Barton, L. (eds) *Disability, Human Rights and Education: Cross-Cultural Perspectives* Buckingham: Open University Press, pp. 87–99.

Rogers, C. (2003) 'The mother/researcher in blurred boundaries of a reflexive research process' *Auto/Biography* XI (1&2), pp. 47–54.

Rogers, C. (2007) 'Experiencing an "inclusive" education: parents and their children with 'special educational needs' *British Journal of Sociology of Education* 28 (1), pp. 55–68.

Rose, N. (1989) *Governing the Soul: The Shaping of the Private Self* London: Free Association Books.

Russell, P. (1997) 'Parents as partners: some early impressions of the impact of the Code of Practice' in Wolfendale, S. (ed.) *Working With Parents of SEN Children After the Code of Practice* London: David Fulton Publishers, pp. 69–81.

Russell, P. (2003a) 'Access and achievement or social exclusion? Are government policies working for disabled children and their families?' *Children & Society* 17, pp. 215–25.

Russell, P. (2003b) 'The expectations of parents of disabled children' *British Journal of Special Education* 30 (3), pp. 144–49.

Seligman, M. and Darling, R. (1997) *Ordinary Families, Special Children: A Systems Approach to Childhood Disability* New York: The Guilford Press.

SENCO-FORUM. (2003a) 'What's in a label?' *British Journal of Special Education* 30 (2), p. 107.

SENCO-FORUM (2003b) 'Do SATs harm children, and are they useful anyway?' *British Journal of Special Education* 30 (3), p. 163.

Shakespeare, T (1994) 'Cultural representation of disabled people: dustbins for disavowal?' *Disability & Society* 9 (3), pp. 283–99.

Shelley, M. (1994 [1818]) *Frankenstein* Berkshire: Penguin Books.

Sibley, D. (1995) *Geographies of Exclusion* London: Routledge.

Silva, E. (ed.) (1996) Good Enough Mothering: Feminist Perspectives on Lone Motherhood London: Routledge.

Simmons, K. (2000) 'Parents, legislating and inclusion' in Daniels, H. (ed.) *Special Education Re-formed Beyond Rhetoric?* London: Falmer Press, pp. 255–67.

Slack, S. (1999) 'I am more than my wheels' in Corker, M. and French, S. (eds) *Disability Discourse* Buckingham: Open University, pp. 28–37.

Smart, C. (1996) 'Deconstructing motherhood' in Bortolaia Silva, E. (ed.) *Good Enough Mothering: Feminist Perspectives On Lone Motherhood* London: Routledge, pp. 37–57.

Smart, C. and Neale, B. (1999) *Family Fragments?* Cambridge: Polity Press.

Smith, D. (1988) *The Everyday World as Problematic: A Feminist Sociology* Milton Keynes: Open University Press.

Sontag, S. (1991) *Illness as Metaphor and AIDS and its Metaphors* London: Penguin Books.

Sparkes, A.C. (1994) 'Life histories and the issue of voice: reflections on an emerging relationship' *Qualitative Studies in Education* 7 (2), pp. 165–83.

Spock, B. (1946/1973) *Baby and Child Care* New York: Duell, Sloan and Pearce.

Stanley, L. (1993) 'On auto/biography in sociology' *Sociology* 27 (1), pp. 41–52.

Stoppard, M. (1984) *The Babycare Book* London: Dorling Kindersley.

Stoppard, M. (1985 [2000]) *Pregnancy and Birth Handbook* London: Dorling Kindersley.

Swain, J. and Cook, T. (2001) 'In the name of inclusion: we all, at the end of the day, have the needs of the children at heart' *Critical Social Policy* 21 (2), pp. 185–207.

Swift, J (1967 [1726]) *Gullivers Travels* Harmondsworth: Penguin Books Ltd.

Tomlinson, S. (1982) *A Sociology of Special Education* London: Routledge & Kegan Paul.

Tozer, R. (1999) *At the Double: Supporting Families with Two or More Severely Disabled Children* London: National Children's Bureau Enterprises Ltd.

Vincent, C. (2000) *Including Parents? Education, Citizenship and Parental Agency* Buckingham: Open University Press.

Walkerdine, V. and Lucey, H. (1989) Democracy in the Kitchen: Regulating Mothers and Socialising Daughters London: Virago.

Wallbank, J. A. (2001) *Challenging Motherhood(s)* Essex: Pearson Education Ltd.

Warren Dodd, L. (2004) 'Supporting the siblings of young children with disabilities' *British Journal of Special Education* 31 (1), pp. 41–9.

Wilson, J. (1999) 'Some conceptual difficulties about "inclusion"' *Support for Learning* 14 (3), pp. 110–12.

Winnicot, D. W. (1964) *The Child, the Family, and the Outside World* London: Penguin.

Winnicot, D. W. (1988) *Babies and Their Mothers* London: Free Association Books Ltd.

Wright Mills, C. (1959) *The Sociological Imagination* New York: Oxford University Press.

Wyness, M. G. (1996) *Schooling, Welfare and Parental Responsibility* London: Falmer Press.

Young, J. (1999) *The Exclusive Society* London: Sage Publications.

# Index